# Painting
## *with*
## Scissors

To your next phase,
All my best - xo
Ann

chief clark.

# Painting
## *with*
# Scissors

*How to use the tools you have
to make your life and work a masterpiece*

Ann Mehl
*and*
Mark McDevitt

Library of Congress Control Number: 2018951480
First Printing, 2018

Mehl, Ann
Painting with Scissors:
How to use the tools you have to make your life and work a masterpiece

ISBN-13: 978-1987590876
ISBN-10: 1987590872

Jacket & Interior Design: Aubree Holliman of AH HA Creative
Author photo: Tina DeAngelis

Printed in the USA by CreateSpace

For more information, please visit
www.annmehl.com

*For Mark and James,*
*who teach me every day what love means.*

# Acknowledgments

This book would not have been possible without the love, support and encouragement of my husband, Mark. It was his creative vision and writerly talent that first set the ball in motion, and keeps it in motion. Thanks to our son James who keeps us permanently running, and reminds us every day how to stay in the moment.

I am also deeply grateful to my parents, Walter and Sally Mehl, who gave me the best possible start in life, and who by their example, showed me the nature of love and commitment.

Last, but certainly not least, I would like to acknowledge all those individuals with whom I've worked over the years, whose trust and hard work makes my job so fulfilling. I hope this book communicates some of the love, pride and gratitude that I feel for you.

# Contents

# Introduction

This is a book largely written by accident. Some time after starting my coaching practice in 2006, I began writing a monthly newsletter, a way to keep in touch with clients and generate potential new business. Over time, I saw its reach steadily grow and through the magic of "forward email," these little missives went out into the world where they introduced me to a raft of new friends and contacts. Nothing makes your day like a kind note from a total stranger, and there were lots of these. They would say things like "Hey, this is great! I sent it to my son, can you add me to your mailing list?" Or, "Hey, do you mind if I print this and share it with my colleagues at work?" Some people encouraged me to write a book, an idea I first thought laughable. But somehow the tiny seed was planted. If you are one of those people, thank you for your interest and encouragement.

My approach to coaching is pretty straightforward. I want people to have a better experience of living, to feel more joy, more connected to themselves and others. To this end, I usually offer up whatever tricks, tools and experience I have learned over the years. I have been fortunate to have some very good teachers but as useful as they are, I often learn as much from my clients. Every day, I am privy to deep, frank, challenging conversations about accomplishment and frustration, success and failure, joy and loss. I have seen clients turn apparent disasters into wins, and transform weaknesses into strengths. I have heard, processed, and reflected back the insights of countless smart, driven professionals over the years, and I am wiser because of it.

The essays in this book are a distillation of some of those conversations which I have grouped together by theme. As with all advice, it is usually autobiographical, in that what I write about is often what I am experiencing or struggling with myself. The magic of the written word is when you share this experience with someone else and they can see themselves in it, taking away something positive from it. My hope is that you will also find some encouragement or inspiration among these pages. Take whatever is useful and disregard the rest.

The title comes from the French painter, Henri Matisse, whose story you'll read about in Chapter 4 (on Courage). When Matisse's eyesight began to fail him, he found an ingenious way to continue his artistic output by using only a scissors and some colored paper. This adaptability and sheer doggedness of will would result in some of his best-loved and most enduring works known as the "Cut Out Series." As advice for living, I can think of no better metaphor.

We all encounter setback and failure at times, and nobody ever has all the tools or resources they need. Life isn't about having the perfect set of conditions. It's about doing the best you can with the available resources. In the words of Teddy Roosevelt: "Do what you can, with what you have, where you are." What you hold in your hands is some of the advice I have given that other people thought was important enough to save or share. For better or worse, here it is, my own rusty pair of scissors. I hope it helps.

—Ann Mehl

# CHAPTER ONE

# The Big Picture

*"My biggest fear was that I would come to the end of my life and discover that I had lived someone else's dream."*

———

**Karen Blixen**

# 200 Words

How do you capture the essence of a life and legacy in about 200 words or less? That is the onerous task—and awesome responsibility—faced every day by the newspaper obituary writer. In the wake of 9/11, the reporters at the *New York Times* faced an even greater challenge. How to memorialize nearly 3000 dead, most of whom were known only to friends and family?

The solution they came up with was to focus each one on a singular story or small idiosyncratic detail that best captured the essence of that person. Thus, the moving "Portraits of Grief" column that ran daily in the *Times* for three and a half months in the wake of that horrific event. It was an impressionistic mosaic of the city that provided an intimate glimpse into the lives of others. For some, it was a too-painful reminder of their lives forever changed. For others, it was a means of connecting with the victims, a source of healing and consolation.

Jan Hoffman wrote more than 75 of these portraits. And what she found most revealing in speaking with their loved ones was that no one ever talked about that person's job. "It was always about love. It was about connection." As she delved into people's lives, she found the things that came to define them usually had very little to do with their work. Inevitably, it was about an undying devotion to a losing baseball team. A daughter's graduation. A beloved pooch rescued from the pound. A family holiday tradition. Love of leopard-skin pants and pink rhinestone-studded sunglasses. In other words, it was about that person's "values."

Mostly what I do as a coach is encourage people to look deeply at their own internal value system to make sure it is properly aligned with their stated priorities. Are the things you are striving for in line with your own deepest held values? Are you being who *you* want to be, or who others want you to be? What would you say are your core principles? Is what you are doing the same as what you are saying? Think of your values as an internal compass, guiding you. If that compass is off by even a few degrees, then every step you take leads you further away from where you really want to go.

The issue, for some of us, is that we are operating for the most part on default settings—a *false* value system inculcated by advertising, poor parenting or whatever forces may have shaped us. Is money your ultimate goal? Is that where you derive meaning in life? Then it's almost certain you will never feel that you have enough. Slavishly worship youth and beauty? Chances are you will continue to feel old and marginalized. Worship power? Then it's unlikely you will ever feel fully secure, and worse, you will need increasingly *more* power to keep the fear at bay. We know this already, we're not dummies. But it's easy to *forget* what really matters in the midst of all of our striving.

How do we find meaning and purpose for our lives? What I would suggest here—and I'm sure Jan Hoffman would agree—is that what really matters in the end is only one thing: the quality of our close relationships with other people. Our friends, our families, our co-workers, our neighbors. This is where we will find the most meaning in our brief, wondrous lives. To this end, I will sometimes have clients write out their own obituary as a "values exercise." And it is surprisingly effective.

In his book, *The 7 Habits of Highly Effective People*, Steven Covey talks about the need to "begin with the end in mind." I'm paraphrasing here, but he says that all things are created twice: first in the mind as a mental picture, and secondly in the physical realm in accordance with that mental map we create. If you don't make a conscious effort to decide what you want out of life, then you run the risk of letting others determine that for you. "Begin with the end in mind" means knowing your desired destination, and then holding yourself accountable to those dreams and that mission.

Years ago, I shared a summer rental with some friends on the Jersey Shore. One of my housemates was a guy named Ron Breitweiser. He died tragically on 9/11. This is how his "portrait" read in the *New York Times*, under the title "A Ring From a Sweetheart."

Ronald and Kristen Breitweiser were married five years ago in bathing suits and bare feet "on a little sand spit in the middle of nowhere," Mrs. Breitweiser recalled. After years of marriage, the two continued to act like newlyweds. Each weekday, Mr. Breitweiser, 39, would return from his job as a senior vice president at Fiduciary Trust International at 2 World Trade Center, sit on the living room couch in their New Jersey house, and snuggle with his wife for a few minutes. They called each other "Sweets."

"I don't think we ever used our real names," recalled Mrs. Breitweiser, who was a lawyer before she gave up her job to raise their daughter, Caroline, who is now 2 and nicknamed Bug, after the way she used to crawl.

When Caroline woke up at night, Mr. Breitweiser would rub her back until she fell asleep. Sometimes he chased the family's golden retriever, Sam, to make her giggle. On Sept. 8, the family went to a nearby beach at Sandy Hook. Mr. Breitweiser pointed to two gray rectangles in the distance. "Look, that's where Daddy works," he said. Some of Mr. Breitweiser's remains, including his wedding ring, were recovered from ground zero in October. The authorities gave Mrs. Breitweiser her husband's ring, which she wears on her right hand. Her own wedding ring stays where it was, on her left. (Profile published in *The New York Times* on March 17, 2002.)

Now ask yourself: "How will they capture my life in 200 words?" Then begin with that end in mind.

# Whose Life Is It Anyway?

ONE OF MY all-time favorite movies is *The Truman Show* starring Jim Carrey. The hero, Truman, lives inside a Utopian bubble carefully constructed for him by a savvy media company. Unbeknownst to Truman, hidden cameras broadcast his every move live on television 24/7 to an audience of millions. While outwardly, he appears happy-go-lucky, inwardly a subtle desperation begins to take hold as he gradually realizes that the life he thought was his, is, in fact a monstrous hoax perpetrated upon him.

On one level, the film is a biting satire of our voyeuristic media-saturated culture. But a more careful examination reveals deep layers of subtext dealing with issues of self-determination and free will. Having finally discovered the true nature of his existence, Truman is faced with a vexing choice: does he choose the false—albeit very comfortable—existence that has been given him, or does he exercise his free-will in choosing a life that is uniquely his own, with all of the attendant uncertainty and risk that real living entails? Happily, he chooses the latter, and in so doing he becomes a "true man."

It's a choice that all of us, sooner or later, must contend with if we are to become truly independent people. While the choice may seem obvious ("Who would want to live like that?"), it's startling just how difficult this can be. I know of a man in his mid 50s who was recently weighing a job opportunity in London. Ultimately, he turned down what was a very lucrative offer when his 90-year-old mother deemed the firm less "prestigious" than the one he was currently with! You may laugh, but it's more common than you think.

Charlie, an attractive investment banker, recently confided in me that he would really like to meet someone. He keeps himself immaculately, owns a beautiful apartment in Manhattan, and what does he do every weekend? He goes home to visit his parents on Long Island. Now, while it's nice that he feels welcome and loved in the bosom of his family, he must also know that this is totally incongruous with his stated goal of meeting someone and having a life of his own. For that, he needs—like Truman—to get outside of his comfort bubble.

The "disease to please" is a common one, and nobody is immune. It is the daughter who marries within the faith though she loves another; the employee who remains stuck in his lowly rank when he knows he is capable of more; the recent grad who applies to business school when she wants to be an artist. It is showing up to an event out of guilt, and then resenting the subtle manipulations that got us there, in which we ourselves are complicit.

But aren't we supposed to be considerate of others? Yes, but our primary responsibility must be for our own happiness. Just as the airlines recommend putting on your own oxygen mask first in case of emergency, so too must you attend to your own needs if you are to be of any use to others. Enlightened self-interest is not selfishness—rather, it is at the very heart of all healthy adult human behavior. As long as you live, you will NEVER EVER please everyone all the time.

I'm not dismissing the very real pressures that many people feel—from parents, peers, society. I watched after my own mother in New Jersey for many years when at times, I resented the obligation. It is difficult to live a life in keeping with your own highest ideals. The voices of opposition can be loud and obnoxious. But there's another voice—maybe not as loud, but altogether more truthful. It's the voice of your own true nature, your essential self.

Signs that you may be ignoring your essential voice may include: boredom, irritability, interrupted sleep or eating habits, self-medicating with drugs or alcohol, reckless behavior which imperils those close to you, extramarital affairs and so on. You may feel you are doing everything right, and yet something feels wrong. This is often the painful place that people are in when they come to me for coaching. While I don't profess to have all the answers, I am very good at asking questions. Here are some that I frequently ask:

1. Where are you stuck in your life and in what way has this "stuckness" cost you dearly?

2. Where are you resistant to change? How has this limited the choices for your life?

3. What is your greatest fear and what is the hard wiring that supports this? Can it be revised?

4. Where are you avoiding necessary conflict in your life, and therefore at war with yourself?

5. Where are you still seeking others' approval? Why are you allowing them to write the script for your life?

In the end, it all comes down to individual choice. Is the life you are living truly yours, or an expression of someone else's dream? In the movie *Out of Africa*, pioneer Karen Blixen confesses: "My biggest fear was that I would come to the end of my life and realize that I had lived someone else's dream."

Only you—like Truman—have the power to choose.

# Three Questions

THERE'S NOTHING QUITE like knowing who you are and what you stand for. One startup clothing company in Brooklyn knows all about this. Last year, their company mission statement—dubbed the "Holstee Manifesto"—accidentally went viral, quickly becoming an internet sensation with more than 50 million views in a couple of months. When Holstee turned that message into a poster, it quickly became one of the company's top sellers. It's full of great lines such as: "Life is about the people you meet and the things you create with them." Notice how people comes before things. I believe this message resonated with the masses because it was a statement of their core values, not a traditional company mission statement. Most company statements all sound alike, because they have very little to do with the actual people who work there.

While manifestos are public declarations of intent, we each have our own "personal" mission, and if we don't, we would do well to consider what that is. A couple of years ago, after my father died, I wrote a short piece about him. He was well-liked in the town of Roseland, New Jersey, where I grew up. A man some people would describe as "salt of the earth." I doubt sincerely if he ever wrote down his beliefs, but he lived by a simple code that defined him. He never had any doubt about who he was (himself), or why he went to work every day (his family). I think one of the major failings of our time is that so many of us live without a clear intent or purpose.

To this end, I will often have clients write out their own personal mission statement. There is no right or wrong way to do it. It's simply an exercise to keep yourself in touch with what's really important to you. For example: I want to be a good husband, mother or father. I want to walk lighter through the world and not take everything so seriously. I want to handle setbacks and crises in a level-headed manner, be less reactive. I want to live courageously and with integrity, critics be damned. The point is to be aware of your higher motives, and then when times get tough, your default programming helps you to stay connected with that better part of yourself. To help in crafting a mission statement, here are three questions that I find useful to ask.

## WHO AM I?

The key here is in knowing what are my "core values." What are the minimum basic standards I expect of myself and others. Knowing these helps me make better decisions on a daily basis. Without knowing these, you can end up appropriating other people's values, until a slow erosion of identity renders you unrecognizable even to yourself. Very important: Do not let other people define your values. You must know what you stand for, and more importantly, what you will *not* stand for. Many people take offense when their values are affronted in some way. But remember, offense is taken, not given. When you are secure in your own personal set of values, no outside forces can sink your boat. In the words of William Ernest Henley from his wonderful poem Invictus: "I am the master of my fate; I am the captain of my soul."

## WHAT DO I WANT?

If you don't know what you want, you usually end up getting a lot of what you don't want. Deep down, most of us know what we really want to have happen. Oftentimes what we lack is the courage of our conviction. We are afraid of not getting it. And how will we cope then? So, better not to even want it, right? Wrong. I see this all the time in my coaching, and what I try to do is leverage the odds that something might be possible. Often that slit of light, that glimmer of hope, is enough to allow our own natural creative instincts to kick in and do the work. Focus on what you want, not what you don't want. Then commit fully to making that happen. Like the old saying: "As you think, so you shall be." Never stop planning. Never stop dreaming. Never stop trying.

## HOW DO I WANT TO BE REMEMBERED?

This is the surest way to figure out how to live well. If we can begin with the end in mind, we will always be guided by our higher values. What legacy do I want to leave behind? What will be my proudest accomplishment? Am I a good partner, a supportive friend, someone who makes the workplace a little better? Do I share my feelings with people openly and honestly? Do I give time to the people who need it? When the temptation is there to act small, think longer term and be the bigger person. Act the way you would want to be remembered.

It's worth taking a few minutes to write out your own personal mission statement. No one has to see it. You can keep it in your wallet or nightstand. When you look at it, let it remind you of the core values that define you. Not only will it guide you, but it may guide others as well.

Who am I? What do I want? How do I want to be remembered?

# No Regrets

**B**RONNIE WARE KNOWS a thing or two about regret. She is a palliative care nurse in Australia who spent years caring for patients in the last moments of their lives. She began documenting some of their dying epiphanies in a blog, which later became a popular book called "The Top Five Regrets of the Dying." In it, she writes of the extreme clarity that many people were able to achieve at the end of their lives, and how we might learn from it.

As you'd expect, common themes emerged from her work with the dying ("I wished I had worked less. I wish I'd stayed in touch with my friends more.") But by far the most common theme was some version of this sentiment: I wish I'd had the courage to live a life true to myself, and not the life others expected of me.

In my coaching practice, I often see people who are dying a little every day because the life they are living on the outside clearly does not match who they are on the inside. They tell me they're exhausted. And I think one of the reasons they're exhausted is that they are not wholehearted about what they are doing. They're doing it because they have an abstract idea that this is what they *should* be doing.

At different times in my own journey, I've felt this disconnect too, and it's painful. It takes constant vigilance and the asking of some difficult questions to live the life we intended. But if we are sincere in the asking, it can lead us to be more courageous, more present, more connected to our lives and the people we share it with. Here are some questions that I use to check in with myself:

1. Where am I not being fully myself? What is the reason for this?

2. Where am I not fully expressing my needs? What is this costing me?

3. Whose approval am I seeking? Why is that person's opinion so important to me?

We all have our public and private selves to some degree. But we need to feel free to be our true selves most of the time, or the weight of the artifice can become exhausting. I had a friend in college who slogged his way through medical school because his father always wanted him to be a doctor. In his second year of medical school, it became clear that the path he was on was not suiting him. He was frequently sick with unexplained maladies, and eventually had to be hospitalized suffering from nervous exhaustion. Thankfully, he was able to talk to his father and admit that while he enjoyed medicine, his real passion was for teaching music. The following year, he changed courses and never looked back. But not before literally making himself sick trying to please someone else.

The disease to please is a common one, and nobody is immune. Many of us are taught early on that the needs of others should always come before our own, and we bend ourselves into pretzels accordingly. Nice girls don't cause a fuss, only selfish people look out for themselves, and so on. But there is nothing enlightened about silently keeping the peace, while quietly giving yourself an ulcer from seething resentment. Learning to express your own needs, clearly and unapologetically, is the first step towards recovery. When we can do this, we become much more pleasant to be around, and more tolerant of others who have needs different from our own.

With the passing of my sister-in-law and both of my parents in recent years, I've looked carefully at my own motivations. I wanted to make sure that the life I was living was fully my own. With practice, I have learned to distinguish between a "should" and "want" statement. "I want to go to the gathering this evening" is always preferable to "I should go to this gathering." One implies choice, the other duty. Notice how any activity that stems from choice feels uplifting, while those that stem from obligation feel deadening. Are you saying yes because you want to, or because you're afraid to say no? There's a world of difference.

In his epic 1915 poem, *The Love Song of J. Alfred Prufrock*, T.S. Eliot gave to the world his most enduring literary creation. Prufrock, the hapless hero, wanders alone through unnamed streets, wrestling with deep existential feelings of loss and regret. His deepest frustration, it seems, stems from what he sees as the inability to clearly articulate himself. Over and over, we get the weary refrain: "No, that is not it at all; that is not what I meant at all." Is the life you are living the one you meant, or is it like Prufrock, a manifestation of someone else's dream?

The people we tend to admire most are the ones who live their lives without apology. We use names like maverick, hero or genius to describe them—never allowing for the possibility that we might become one of them. But why couldn't we? Once we recognize that our time here is finite, we are less driven by the distraction of external voices. What can you choose to do right now, so that years from now, when you're looking back at your path, you might feel genuine pride? These are the decisions your future self will thank you for.

# Scar Tissue

O N SEPTEMBER 22, 2010, my mom, Sally Ann Mehl, died of complications from cancer. She was 75 years old. She died at home in our "living room," propped up in a rented hospital bed.

There was very little warning. A fortnight before she died, my mom and I attended a birthday party for my Uncle Pete. We laughed with our relatives, ate eggplant parm and ice-cream cake (her favorite). In the two weeks that followed, we learned that my mother had cancer of the gall bladder, which had metastasized into her liver. What should have been a routine operation to remove troublesome gall stones turned into a ten-day hospital vigil of hushed conversations, hand-wringing, dwindling options—finally ending with that execrable phrase "take her home, make her comfortable." Her only choice in the end was where she would die. Since she was not lucid, my siblings and I made that decision for her and took her back to our house in Roseland.

The facts of my mother's life are as unremarkable as cancer. She was born, lived and died in New Jersey. She never went to college, wrote an autobiography, or took home an Oscar. She never appeared on television, traveled to Africa or won a Nobel Peace Prize. In fact, she rarely ever won the raffle during the local church fund-raising night. But she did take the prize in one category: mother. She excelled at it, and she cherished being a mom and grandmother. She took great pride in telling anyone who would listen, "I have five kids." Or more specifically, "I've got five great kids."

She was a woman who knew and accepted her own limitations. She didn't have to be Wonder Woman like we all do now. When she didn't know the answers to questions we'd ask, she'd buy *Tell Me Why* reference texts and encyclopedias to help us stretch our minds beyond her own understanding of the world. She made flashcards for me when I struggled with the multiplication tables. She could whip up a mean Taylor ham and egg sandwich. My mom preserved our first grade book reports and school papers in a file cabinet like they were the Dead Sea Scrolls. Mrs. Mehl had a special knack for sewing and making meatball sandwiches for the students at Our Lady of Blessed Sacrament. Our Halloween costumes were always the most fabulous, and always completely homemade.

The last few days while my mother was in the hospital, we spent the time talking and holding hands. We cried a little. She told me her stories, the same ones she has recited a thousand times over (she also had Alzheimer's). She gave me kisses and winks. I thanked her for loving me.

While emotionally draining, the experience of walking with someone on the last leg of this journey is an absolute privilege. Being present to my mom in these moments taught me more about letting go, grace, patience and sacrifice than all of the meditation, marathon running, psychotherapy and yoga that I've done in the last ten years combined. In her book *Stitches*, Anne Lamott says something like this: "Ultimately, we are all here just walking each other home."

That's not to say I'm fine with it all. I'm not. Two weeks' notice is simply not enough. Yes, I'm glad that my mom's suffering is over;

she had a lot of pain towards the end. And I'm glad that the dementia that slowly stripped away her memory and dignity over the last six years is now powerless against her. But I'm mad that she will never know my son or attend my brother's wedding next month. I feel cheated when I see others walking the planet who have given up on themselves while my mom wasn't given another month to watch the leaves turning this Fall. But this kind of thinking gets you nowhere.

I've noticed too that people behave in the oddest ways when you are bereaved. That's okay, most people don't know what to do. And yet, kind words are a huge consolation. So if someone you know is grieving, say something, even if it's "I don't know what to say." It's nice when someone stops by to drop off a prayer blanket in the mailbox outside, but far better to come inside and sit for a few minutes. Touch the person. Talk to them. Say nothing at all.

And therein lies the rub: most of us are simply terrified of death, even more so of sickness. Seeing it, being near it, watching someone else go through it—it's uncomfortable. But why? Isn't this the one experience that unites us all in the end? This isn't to be morbid about it, or to feel superior in my grief —"you haven't lived what I've gone through." But when you see the lengths to which people will go in order to avoid facing their own mortality, you realize just how silly it all is. Our time here is finite. And very short. The trick is to use that knowledge to your advantage. All that worry and guilt and anxiety that consumes you from day to day—guess what? It's useless and doesn't serve you. Wasted human energy. Norman Cousins said it best: "Death is not the greatest loss in life. The greatest loss is what dies inside us while we are still living."

If my mom showed me anything, it is the enduring value of friendships. The route to a meaningful life does not lie in the accumulation of "stuff"—but in the quality of the relationships you cultivate along the way. The outpouring of affection for her in the past few weeks has been consoling and beautiful. And she deserves all of it, because she gave so much of it herself. I'm reminded of that great Beatles line: "And in the end, the love you get is equal to the love you give."

People tell you time heals all wounds. Letting go is never easy, but holding on is harder. And on and on. I know these quotes and use them myself from time to time. But the one I like most is: "Scar tissue is stronger than regular tissue. Realize its strength; move on."

The funny thing is, you know very quickly when something like this happens whether you are going to be okay or not. And even in my initial shock at the hospital, I had a feeling that everything was going to be okay. Yes, there will be sadness ahead, scar tissue, feelings of loss. But everything is going to be okay. It already is.

Sally Ann Mehl 1935–2010

R.I.P

# CHAPTER TWO

# Self-Love

*"Love yourself first and everything else falls into line.*
*You really have to love yourself*
*to get anything done in this world."*

—

**Lucille Ball**

# Running On Empty

ONE OF THE most common refrains I hear as a corporate coach is, "I'm just too busy!" What used to be called overworked is now called crazybusy, slammed, swamped, jammed, maxed-out—or God help us—no more bandwidth!

Anyone who owns a car understands that it takes regular maintenance to keep it on the road. You don't ignore warning lights or drive it with the needle in the red all the time—or if you do, you won't stay on the road very long. If you own a car, chances are you change the oil every 3000 miles, rotate the tires every now and then, maybe even take it for a tune-up now that Spring is here. Yet, we think nothing of driving ourselves this way without any fuel whatsoever—and then somehow act surprised when we end up in the ditch with our wheels spinning.

Burnout can be described as a state of mental, physical and emotional exhaustion. Symptoms may vary, but the signs you're headed for a crash are not all that hard to recognize: difficulty concentrating on simple tasks, difficulty sleeping even when you're exhausted, feeling sad or hopeless about the future, feeling disconnected from friends and loved ones, feeling that no one else but you can do the job.

# MANAGE YOUR ENERGY, NOT YOUR TIME

The conventional wisdom emphasized managing your time effectively as the key to staying on course. But as the pace of communication and the demands of the workplace increase, the tendency is for us to work more and more hours to keep up—which can often lead to burnout. Time is a finite resource; but the energy we need to perform the work is renewable. And this is what we need to protect.* The key here is learning to properly recharge after the expenditure of energy. Watch any professional tennis player and witness the perfect management of human energy. Point, rest, point, rest. What you see in between points—the ritual tweaking of strings, the automatic relaxation of muscles—this is all learned behavior designed to maximize performance and concentration.

# REPLENISH THE WELL

Governments have long had fishing quotas in place to prevent overfishing from depleting the seas of their natural resource. Farmers, too, understand the necessity of crop rotation in order to prevent the soil being stripped of its essential nutrients. The same holds true for us. We need to protect and replenish our own wellsprings of energy or the well may dry up. Sadly, the average American vacation is now down to a long weekend (compared to Australians who have over 3 weeks and Europeans with 4-5 weeks paid vacation). If you can't afford 4 weeks to go hiking in the Himalayas, just taking regular mini-breaks throughout the day can help. Engage in a 10-minute pause from whatever you are working on and do something completely different. Unplugging from technology—even if it's just for fifteen minutes at a time—can also be enormously liberating. Your own well of energy is your most precious natural resource. Learn to protect it.

## FIND YOUR PLAY

It's harder and harder as we get older to hold onto the idea of play as something that is useful. But play is more than just a frivolous childhood pastime. As adults, it is essential that we have activities in which we can lose ourselves completely once in a while. Play allows us to recharge without having to "perform" or attain results. It's no accident that some of the most brilliant minds are sometimes described as being "childlike" (The Dalai Llama and Albert Einstein). Anything that causes you to lose track of time is an activity worth pursuing. And it's different for everyone. I read in an interview recently that Rod Stewart has a thing for model railways. He has a whole ballroom devoted to it! For others it's a good book, planting a garden or painting a flower. You don't even have to be good at it, just so long as you enjoy it. Years ago, I went to a beginner's surf camp in Mexico. Here, I learned that the best surfer is the one having the most fun.

## JOIN A SUPPORT GROUP

Sure you can go it alone, but you don't have to. For human beings to be truly healthy, we need to feel like we are a part of something bigger than just ourselves. A leaf off the tree has the advantage of floating wherever it wants, but once disconnected from the tree, it quickly dies. You have to be both an individual—to have a sense that you are fully unique—and you also need to feel connected to a bigger organism—a family, a community, a club, a tribe. There are people out there with invaluable information and experience who are eager to share it with you—all you have to do is pick up the phone. Research has shown that there is a direct correlation between our physical health and community. Having people around you who make you feel vibrant, alive and hopeful can literally add years to your life.

Proper rest, nutrition, exercise, play, community—we know what we need. So don't ignore the warning lights on the dash when they come on. Regular maintenance is always cheaper than a major overhaul.

* The idea of "energy management" comes from the Human Performance Institute®, and its founder, Tony Schwartz.

# In Good Company

As a coach for Girls On The Run, one of the lessons I try to instill in the girls who participate in the program is the importance of positive self-image. For girls at this formative age (8-14), it's absolutely critical that their inner dialogue be constructive. As a wise woman said to me once in a yoga class: "You only get one body in this lifetime and it's a good idea to make friends with it, or you're in for a very rough ride."

Like your body, your internal dialogue is your constant traveling companion. And that conversation had better be friendly or you'll be faced with a lifetime of pain. Negative self-talk can be brutal, and nothing robs people of their health and happiness faster. Yet most of us are unaware of the power of that voice because it happens so subtly. Before I even get out of bed in the morning, I will have a dozen automatic thoughts, none of them helpful. Now that I've slept past the alarm, I'll never make it. I have nothing to offer today. Help, I'm in over my head!

Sound familiar? Most people, if they're honest, can usually pinpoint one or two specific ongoing debates they are engaged in. Common thematic threads include: I'm lousy at my job, I can't believe no one has actually noticed yet. I will never accomplish anything worthwhile with my life. I have no discernible skills. Look at me, I'm too old, middle-aged and tired. I am unattractive, nobody will ever want me. This is not acceptable.

Now, imagine for a second, a friend saying that to you. How would you feel? That person would no longer be your pal, right? Yet, we do this to ourselves every single day.

But we don't have to. Like all bad habits, the tendency to react with harsh, self-directed criticism is one that can be unlearned. The first step is awareness. Like tuning into the signal of an obscure AM radio station, you may have to listen carefully at first to locate the source of this verbal abuser. It's important to remember that this is not some oracle of truth. It's just a bunch of noise and tired old jingles you forgot to erase a long time ago. But remember, you own the radio. So if you don't like what you're hearing, change the channel. Or simply toss it out.

Here are some strategies I use/recommend for creating a more constructive inner dialogue.

## THE 8-MINUTE SOLUTION

Find a place where you'll be undisturbed for 8 minutes. During this brief time, I want you to write down examples of occasions when: someone loved or praised you, even though you didn't perform perfectly; evidence of when your work received recognition; ways that you've added value or acted courageously. If you're deeply mired in self-loathing, this is not easy. Do it anyway—for eight full minutes. You're pushing yourself to make new associations—unthinking the painful and imprisoning thoughts you're more used to. Next week, do it again. If you talk back to your inner critic, it very quickly begins to lose steam. It doesn't like the competition.

# BAIT AND SWITCH

By repeating any negative messages to yourself, you can easily create a limiting belief that becomes a self-fulfilling prophecy. The trick is to catch yourself in the act of doing this, interrupt the irrational fears, and then substitute them with more positive, self-supporting statements. E.G. "What if I stumble on my way up to the podium? What if they see my hands shaking? I know my voice is quavering." That is your inner critic, caught mid-act. Now, substitute that with a more supporting, truthful dialogue: "It's okay, I've done this dozens of times before. So what if I appear nervous, isn't everybody?" Finally, release with a positive affirmation that this is already so: "I am calm and in control" or "It is all happening perfectly."

# JUST ONE THING

You know the voice that says, "game over" before the game has even begun? It makes you feel hopeless and helpless by telling you things will never improve. And that light at the end of the tunnel? Probably a train. This self-defeating voice says things like, "I feel exhausted today, so what's the point in doing anything?" Just whittle it down to size. Breaking any proposed task down into its component parts will combat the tendency to overwhelm yourself. A new exercise program you wish to begin? Start with something very simple—a twenty-minute walk, for example. Then build slowly on that. It doesn't matter what you do, as long as you do *something*. Doing just one thing will combat the tendency to obsess on negative thoughts or debate the futility of action.

## PICTURE A LOVED ONE

If you're having trouble finding something good to say about yourself, picture someone else doing it. How would your best friend, brother, sister, mentor, grandmother describe you to another? Then allow yourself to trust in that person's good opinion of you. The key here is learning to be more gentle and compassionate company for ourselves. By constantly criticizing, we reject not only ourselves, but all of those people who love and care about us as well. Silencing the inner critic may take some work at first. But with practice and awareness, you can change both the way you think *and* feel on a regular basis.

# Bounce

W HEN STAFF SERGEANT Luke Murphy drove into Baghdad in 2006, he lost more than his vehicle. The roadside IED that exploded under his armored car also took away his right leg below the knee. When he got home, Luke became very depressed. He eventually found hope and help with a soldier's survivors network called The Wounded Warrior Project. Now, seven years and 28 surgeries later, he has graduated from Florida State University, is a successful realtor and motivational speaker. "It's not about what you can't do," he says. "It's what you *can* do. I can complain about not having a leg, or I can do something about it and make the best of what I've got."

Thankfully, few of us will ever experience this kind of life-altering trauma. But we all experience loss of some kind. From minor every day changes, to the loss of a job, a home, a loved one, our youth and eventually our independence. What is it that makes some people bounce back from adversity, while others remain stuck? Resilience is the term often used by psychologists to describe this particular quality, and it turns out that human beings show remarkable ability to adapt, even in the face of devastating tragedies. While people vary dramatically in their coping skills, researchers have identified some key factors that contribute to overall resilience when confronted with a crisis

1.  **Strong Social Support**

    The single most important determinant of resilience is the strength of our social support network. Friends, family, co-workers, support groups, online discussion boards—all can be potential sources of social connectivity. Whenever you're dealing with a problem, it is important not to isolate, but to share it with others. Especially with others who may understand the specifics of what you're dealing with—like The Wounded Warrior Project, say. Even when there is no support available, resilient people often develop their own means of communicating. Prisoners in solitary confinement, for example, will sometimes devise a simple "tap code" to communicate with fellow prisoners. That simple tap code becomes a lifeline.

2.  **Getting Up Quickly**

    Resilient people are generally quicker to get back up, once knocked down. They tend not to wallow in it. After a period of adjustment, they look at the available options, and choose one. Sometimes it may be the only option. On the Jersey shore, it is the decision to "rebuild" after Hurricane Sandy struck. Post 9-11 in New York, it is David Letterman going back on TV to tell silly jokes. In *Silver Linings Playbook*, it is the crazy dancing at the end, laughing in the face of mental illness. What resilient people understand is that taking any action—even if it is the wrong one—is usually better than doing nothing at all. Because action focuses our attention and harnesses the energy we need to begin again.

3.  **Identifying as a Survivor, Not a Victim**

    When dealing with any catastrophic event, it is the people who see themselves as "survivors"—rather than victims—who tend to fare better. They have what psychologists call an "internal locus of control." They acknowledge that while bad things can sometimes happen, they generally believe that their life is ultimately not determined by outside forces. They feel as though they are in control of their own destiny, and refuse to be defined by any singular event. Of course, some factors are simply beyond our personal control, like natural disaster, illness, or a roadside bomb. But what resilient people understand is that whatever happens to us, we still have the ability to choose how we will react.

### 4.  Optimism

Another characteristic of resilience is the belief that while life is full of challenges, it is still a game worth playing. And even if things look pretty grim right now, the sun will eventually come out again. Another word for it is hope. Psychologist Martin Seligman, pioneer of the "Positive Psychology" movement, is widely regarded as one of the leading experts on learned helplessness and depression. Optimists, he says, see setbacks as temporary and isolated events. Pessimists tend to see difficulties as fixed and unending, which can lead to a state of learned helplessness. What's the point in doing anything if it's never going to change anything?

From his research, Seligman determined that the state of helplessness was a learned phenomenon. If it could be learned, he reasoned, it could also be unlearned. That is to say, we can learn to be more optimistic. By learning to recognize our thought patterns, interrupt the "negative loop" and replace it with something more helpful, we can grow our resilience muscles.

This is not to diminish or belittle the very real pain that many people face. Probably the most common cause of depression is pain that a person can't fully let go of. And there are many reasons for this. Many people can't let go of old pain, because the only way to do that is to properly feel it. They keep the pain alive, oddly enough, by not letting it in. And so, a moment from the past shapes their lives, and because they have not dealt with it, they are crippled by it.

Having pain in your past or present doesn't make you weak or damaged. It makes you normal. While the situation may be unavoidable, you can grow your resilience muscles and stay focused on a positive outcome.

Remember: it's not about what you can't do, it's about what you *can* do.

# Some People Are Hard on Themselves

Aﬀﬁﬀﬁﬀ FTER A VERY long day at work, I stood in line at the counter waiting for my takeout pizza to bring home. Unconsciously, I was berating myself for all the things I had left undone: taxes still to be filed, an offsite meeting to be prepared, client emails to be returned and all the usual turmoil of an overtired brain. Looking up, I noticed a collection of school essays pinned to the wall, each one proudly displaying a gold star from some unidentified English teacher. This one spoke directly to me, so naturally I took out my phone and took a photograph of it. Here is what it read:

*People Are Hard on Themselves*
*By Sophie B., 4th Grade*

*I have been noticing people being hard on themselves. This is like a little fish swimming into the mouth of a shark. People do this when they meet someone new, when they are trying to impress someone, or when they are trying to learn something new. People are very hard on themselves when they try to impress someone. There she is, I thought in my head. My old ballet teacher was standing right in front of me. Try not to mess up! a voice in my head said.*

*Some people are hard on themselves when they have a friend over that they haven't seen in a long time. And people are hard on themselves when they meet someone new. For example, one time in third grade, a new girl came in the middle of the year. I wanted so bad to impress her. At recess, I started following her everywhere. Even in the cafeteria. Remember to be nice to her, I said to myself. When people meet someone new, they can be real hard on themselves.*

*Also, people can be real hard on themselves when they are learning something new. Ugh! I thought, as I clutched my head that hurt from thinking too hard about the homework that I didn't get. I dropped my pencil, and plopped myself down on the couch. You can be too hard on yourself when you are doing something new and hard. People are hard on themselves for many reasons.*

The first thing that struck me about this essay, aside from how absolutely charming it is, was how well developed this little girl's internal critic is at only 9 years of age. There she is, telling herself not to "mess up" in front of her old ballet teacher. There she is trying desperately to make a "good impression" on the new girl, even following her into the cafeteria. But I especially love the image of her flopping onto the couch, when her head starts to hurt from overthinking her homework. With a cold compress to soothe her addled brain, no doubt!

By the time we reach adulthood, most of us are experts at self-criticism. Why wouldn't we be? We've had years of practice. And we live in a society that loves to judge people harshly and quickly. Look at any hour of network television—the whole world divided into winners and losers. Look at cable news where only the shrillest voices can be heard, and you'll know exactly what I'm talking about. It's no surprise then, that we tend to treat ourselves with the same all-or-nothing approach. If I make a mistake, then I *am* the mistake. If I say something stupid, then I *am* stupid. The seeds are planted early. Poor Sophie here is just getting started.

Negative self-talk is a kind of inner violence that we inflict upon ourselves. And because it happens so quickly and automatically, it tends to go unchallenged. I think if most people were to audit their inner dialogue for just one day, they would be truly shocked at what they're saying to themselves. What does this violence look like? Well, it's ruminating over old mistakes. It's setting standards of perfection that are unattainable, and then beating yourself up when those standards are not met. It's not being patient with yourself when attempting to learn something new or difficult. It's trying to impress someone whose opinion of us we know shouldn't really matter. It's neglecting to appreciate how far you've come. It's not asking for help when you need it.

Some people are very hard on themselves, or "little fish swimming into the mouth of the shark," as Sophie so delicately puts it. So maybe we need to lighten up, cut ourselves some slack now and again. Maybe some of that energy we spend beating ourselves up, we can put into practicing self-compassion. So you screwed up, now what? What did you learn from it? One side benefit of practicing self-compassion is that it can also help our "other" relationships immeasurably too. We are nicer to be around. The more we can forgive ourselves for not being perfect, the more likely we are to be forgiving of others.

When feeling stressed or overwhelmed, we would do well to follow Sophie's example. Drop the pencil, flop onto the couch and apply a cold compress if necessary. The harsh inner critic may never go away, but we don't always have to listen to it. Maybe we can replace the message with something more loving and self-supporting. How about this one: "I am trying to do my best here. And maybe just for today, that's good enough."

Some people are very hard on themselves. Remember to go easy.

*I am not the mistake!*

7/25/11

# Excess Baggage

I HAVE A CLIENT who recently stepped back into the dating pool after enduring a painful breakup. She's smart, witty and attractive—a real "catch" by anyone's standards. She tried online dating for a while with less than stellar results. She confessed that she found the first few dates awkward and stressful, probably because she attached a lot of weight to their successful outcome. "It's exhausting," she said. "It just feels like I'm on a really hard job interview, trying not to step on any landmines." When we met again before the holidays, I asked how things were going and she seemed more optimistic. "I'm letting go of all my expectations," she said. "I've decided I don't want to carry all my old worries forward. From now on, I just want to have fun."

Fear comes in many guises, most of them not helpful for dating, or living. It can look like extreme busyness, total self-sufficiency, trying too hard to impress. All too often we carry it around like a heavy suitcase, laden with the broken pieces of past failures or missed opportunities. One way to reclaim our freedom is to let go of our expectations that things (or people) should be a certain way. Then most everything that happens will come as a welcome surprise.

Every day, we are faced with a similar choice between love and fear—the two most powerful forces in the world. While fear certainly has its uses, it can often keep us from living fully in the present. It also keeps the best part of ourselves unknown. Imagine if we could step out from the shadow of our fears, and live only in love—what would that look like? Would we still be doing what we're doing? Living where we're living? It's worth imagining. But in order to do that, we first need to drop some of our old baggage, and leave it firmly behind. How do we do that?

## I LIKE MYSELF UNCONDITIONALLY, YES!

It's a fundamental truth that we can only truly love and respect another person to the degree that we love and respect ourselves. A healthy self-love is the foundation upon which all our relationships are built—and without which they crumble. This is not egotism or narcissism, but an acceptance of all our strengths and weaknesses. It's about learning to be a good friend, first and foremost to yourself, with all of the leeway and understanding you would grant to someone you value and care about. Not when I lose 10 lbs, or when I find the right mate—but right now, in this very moment. The more we can like ourselves, the more we can love others, and overlook their failings too.

## I FORGIVE MYSELF

We all make mistakes or we wouldn't be human. But without the benefit of a time-machine, there's no going backwards. So be careful what you carry forward. All the half-assed efforts, broken promises, wasted time and energy of the prior year—all of them exist where you can no longer exert influence. Learn from them, grieve for them if you have to, but then tee up the next shot. This is not meant to relinquish you from responsibility, it is in fact making you more responsible, but in a more forward-focused and positive way. Accept that sometimes even your best efforts will fall short, and then strive to do better.

## I LET GO

Once you accept that you are not in charge, no matter how much you want to be, you immediately increase your odds of a favorable outcome. All stress, all strife is the result of a collision between how we think things should be, and how they really are. By trying to accept the reality of human experience, we can save ourselves a lot of grief. While my client has not yet met her Prince Charming, by letting go of some of her expectations, she has opened herself up to a world of new people and experiences.

## I TRY TO HAVE FUN

Set your goals for the year and try to achieve them, but remember that the process is as apt to produce enjoyment as the end product. Look at your habitual patterns of behavior, and ask yourself which ones produce a feeling of contentment, and which ones bring you closer to despair. As simple as it may sound, happiness comes from choosing more of the activities that we know will bring us closer to joy. Anything that gets in the way of that is excess baggage, and needs to be left behind.

May you travel light and have fun getting there.

# CHAPTER THREE

# Fear

*"Fear is the cheapest room in the house.
I would like to see you living in better conditions."*

Hafiz

7/25/19

# Leap of Faith

Last month, I lined up for the Boston Marathon, running on behalf of the Run For Research Team (thank you to all those who kindly donated). What amazes me is that even though I've run this race before and have completed dozens of other marathons in the past, still, there is always that tiny seed of doubt right before the gun goes off. Some little part of me that does not fully believe I can finish the distance ahead of me. Sure, it says, maybe you crossed the finish line before, but what have you got today?

I believe all worthwhile endeavors are like this.

And the more important that challenge is to you, the greater the doubt and risk of failure will be. The Wright Brothers did not know for certain that manned flight was possible before they actually did it. A series of near fatal disasters and financial setbacks preceded their eventual success. But on the morning of December 17th 1903, with a few jerky movements, Orville Wright finally coaxed the ungainly "Wright Flying Machine" into the air. It was a courageous leap of faith that lasted all of twelve seconds, covering a distance of only 120 feet. But it changed forever the course of history.

Anyone who has ever climbed a mountain, started a company or entered a marriage will probably tell you the same thing—you go on faith. Nothing is guaranteed. Sure you may do your homework, develop a brilliant business plan and do background checks, but in the end—you still have to launch that old jalopy into the sky on just a wing and a prayer.

I believe that most people who fail, do so because their leap of faith is underpowered. Nothing is as crippling to human enterprise as this tendency to doubt in our own abilities. If you vacillate for even a second or look down mid-leap, you end up like Wile E. Coyote as he's suspended over the edge of the canyon, legs pumping, before plummeting straight to earth.

How many times have you had a brilliant idea, only to dismiss it out of hand because you're sure someone else has dreamt of it already? Then, after mulling over it for a full year, you see your idea perfectly executed by that someone else. Or how about the attractive stranger across the room you're thinking about approaching? So you stall and bide your time, waiting for just the right moment to make your approach. And before you know it, that moment—and the mysterious stranger have both vanished. Whether you're embarking on a new relationship, looking for a job, or starting a new business, remember this: The leap comes first. Belief comes second. To ensure your leap of faith is not underpowered...

## KNOW WHAT YOU WANT

You really can get there from here, but only if you know where there is. What is it that you really want for yourself in this lifetime? Not what your parents want for you, or your friends, or what you *think* you should want. Only you know the answer to this. Hard to hit the target if it's moving. Nearly impossible if you don't even know where the target is.

## KNOW WHY YOU WANT IT

More important than the what, is the why. What is the feeling that you would have if you were to finally make that leap? Is it confidence? Self-respect? Sovereignty? Freedom? Focusing on your why is more powerful than willpower, coercion or any drill sergeant yelling in your ear. It means your actions are in line with your deepest held values. This is your why.

## SEE IT DONE

I do a lot of work with clients on visualization, because it's powerful and it works. Writing a vision statement opens the door for new possibilities to enter. When making a leap, it's important to focus on the outcome that you want, not the outcome you don't want. Using the leap analogy, it means looking to where you're going to land, not down below into the gaping void.

One of my favorite books from childhood was (and still remains) *The Little Engine That Could*. When all the other "bigger" engines are asked to pull the train, and all for various reasons refuse—it is the Little Blue Engine who takes up the challenge. The Little Engine does not know it can do this, but by repeating its mantra of "I-think-I-can, I-think-I-can" the Engine eventually succeeds in getting the toys over the mountain, congratulating itself on the way down with "I-thought-I-could, I-thought-I-could."

It's alright to be fearful and doubtful. But courage begets more courage. Once you commit and stop hesitating, providence often moves in. And little steps become bigger steps. That's how you finish the Boston Marathon. And that's how you get the toys over the mountain.

# The Monster Under the Bed

O NE OF MY clients, Ed, a sales manager, came to see me in a state of barely-controlled panic. A recent round of layoffs at his company had left him with fewer sales agents and even greater demands for bottom-line results, for which he felt personally responsible. "I know there's pressure in every job," he said. "But this feels like I'm literally drowning." As we got into the session, he confessed that he had been experiencing panic attacks at home, when he was supposed to be away from work and relaxing. As he explained it: "I'm just tired of being scared all the time. I am tired of being afraid."

Fear is a part of our biological makeup, hardwired through millions of years of evolution to keep us safe from extinction. Some fears are probably very healthy, like the fear of snakes or poisonous spiders or woolly mammoths. But many others serve only to keep us stuck—robbing us of our health and happiness. Fear of losing our job. Fear of failure. Fear of success. Fear of unworthiness. Fear of rejection. Fear of terrorism. Fear of aloneness. Fear of illness. Fear of losing the people we love. Fear of death. This is the quotidian stuff that most of us are working with all the time. When it comes up, it's important to remember that we are not drowning, or going crazy. Fear is simple evidence that we are human. What's important is how we handle that fear.

And how do we do that? Well, too often we seek to numb, distract or run away from it—also known as the path of least resistance. A holiday in Mexico, an expensive pair of shoes or a spanking new widescreen television can do wonders to distract us from our fears. But will they alleviate our suffering when the suitcases are unpacked and the novelty of the new TV has worn off? Probably not. Most of us will do anything to avoid the terrible discomfort of confronting our most deeply held fears. But whenever we give in to that impulse, our life shrinks a little bit more. Every time we give in to fear, we cease to truly live. What can we do to alleviate some of this suffering?

## NEVER WORRY ALONE

90% of all our fears are born of loneliness and fatigue. There's a remedy for that. Get some proper rest and reach out to someone—a coach, mentor, support group—anyone who will listen without judgment about what you are currently experiencing. Resist the temptation to push people away while you "get your head together." It's very important that you don't isolate, or you will lose perspective, get depressed or make bad decisions. If you're sharing with friends, just make sure it's an even exchange. Nobody wants to be dumped on all the time, but a good friend is the one who lets you be yourself, in whatever mood you come. We may not always be able to change a particular circumstance or set of facts, but with the perspective of another trusted person, you may choose a different interpretation of those facts.

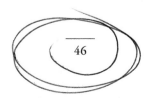

# WRITE IT DOWN

*answere!* (handwritten)

Ask yourself, "What am I afraid of?" Then write it all down. Nobody ever has to read it but you—so make a list. By naming the unnamable, it will automatically lose half its power over you. Do this over a couple of days if necessary. But don't be afraid to look it in the eye. Do you notice any thematic thread to some of these fears? Can you just sit with your worries and look at them in a direct, compassionate, and objective way? Like a reporter trying to understand a story? You don't have to have any big answers right away, but the very act of naming something can be enormously liberating. The monster lurking under the bed is always more frightening than the one we can see standing right in front of us. *expose the monster— name it!!* (handwritten)

# WORST CASE SCENARIO

Our most primal fear is that of losing safety, because safety is fundamental to our survival. Safety means our home, our source of income. The limbic part of our brain—the reptilian lizard brain—is very good at detecting these threats. But in most cases, these threats to our perceived "safety" are largely without merit. So you lose your job, now what? Ask yourself what is the worst thing that can possibly happen here? Go on, imagine it. Prepare yourself to accept this, if necessary, and then calmly try to improve on that situation. Most of these scenarios, if they were to occur, are never as catastrophic as we imagine them to be. If "it" happens, you'll deal with it. But the act of trying to control variables beyond our control is what robs us of present moment enjoyment and fulfillment.

## TAKE ACTION

It's critical that we learn to distinguish between healthy and unhealthy fears. Healthy fears are those that keep us alert and motivated. Unhealthy fears—those whose outcome we cannot affect—tend to cause paralysis and depression. They do not allow for growth. Learning to identify and LET GO of these unhealthy fears, we can then turn our attention to constructive solutions for those outcomes we can affect. Indecision often fertilizes fear so any measure of action taken, however miniscule, is worthwhile.

When facing a predicament ask yourself, "What can I try to do to correct the situation?" Gradually you'll gain momentum. A good plan today is better than a perfect plan tomorrow. So resolve to put your energies into creating mini-goals, and then get busy. It's almost impossible to worry while you are preoccupied doing something that requires planning and thinking.

Fear is not the enemy. But how we handle it can make the difference between a life of fulfillment and a diminished life of quietly suffering desperation. The choice is always ours to make. If you need help to combat the fear, there are a number of options to choose from.

In the words of Hafiz, the Sufi teacher and poet: "Fear is the cheapest room in the house. I want to see you living in better conditions."

# The Discomfort Zone

CHRISTOPHER WAS AN intelligent 41-year-old accountant when he came to me looking to "re-brand" himself in the second half of his life. Though he had a steady, well-paying job, he longed to work as an entrepreneur. Single and attractive, he was still optimistic about meeting a romantic partner, and hopefully one day starting a family. He was excited about the new direction his life was taking, and impatient to begin it immediately. All good indicators that he was serious about change. As a beginning exercise, I suggested he write a business plan with an executive summary, and come up with 3 ideas for ways to meet new people.

When we met again two weeks later, he was still excited but admitted he had been "crazy busy" at work, and hadn't managed to do any writing. Nor had he identified any social opportunities that might allow him to meet single women. I made a few simple suggestions, all of which were rebutted for various reasons: "Too expensive. Too difficult. Too contrived. Too awkward." He was paying me to help him reach his goals, and yet, categorically refusing to do anything that could increase his odds of achieving them. This is one of the most maddening and paradoxical aspects of human nature. We know what it is we need to do to reach our goals, but most of the time, we refuse to do anything that will help us get there. Why? Because we are afraid of the pain.

With Chris, it was the pain of being exposed to criticism or feeling vulnerable that made him avoid writing a business plan, or seek out any interactions with new people. But he paid a heavy price for this, as we all do, when we refuse to leave the comfort of our little magic bubbles. It wouldn't matter if we avoided these things once or twice a year. But for some of us, avoidance becomes a way of life. We barricade ourselves behind a protective wall and rarely venture out because beyond that wall is pain. The comfort zone isn't so much a physical space; it is a mental and psychic prison of our own making. In extreme cases, a person may even hide behind the actual walls of their home, a painful condition known as agoraphobia.

In their new book, *The Tools*, authors Phil Stutz and Barry Michels outline their theory of pain avoidance, and offer practical tools to counter it. Pain avoidance, they argue, has become the central organizing principle of our lives. But escaping pain isn't enough. We also insist on replacing it with pleasure. Internet surfing, shopping, recreational drugs, alcohol, and the aptly named "comfort food"— all keep us happily narcotized and safely at arms length from our true wants and desires. Your comfort zone is supposed to keep you safe—but what it really does is make your life small.

## GETTING BEYOND THE BUBBLE

To take advantage of the endless possibilities that life offers, we have to venture out. But the very first thing we encounter is pain, which sends us scuttling right back to the safety of the comfort zone. The answer put forward by Stutz and Michels is a conscious *choosing* of the pain that negates its power over us—a technique they call

"Reversal of Desire." It's a form of mental conditioning that allows you to move *towards* pain that you know may be beneficial for you.

Think of something that is painful for you. It could be as simple as a phone call you've been putting off, a project that feels overwhelming, or a task that feels tedious and unrewarding. Most people would agree that the temporary discomfort we feel by executing on these, is actually far less than the long-term pain associated with their avoidance. As you move towards it, pain shrinks. When you move away from it, pain grows.

Christopher, while clearly unhappy about his current situation, was unable or unwilling to confront the pain that might allow him to improve upon it. That's okay. Many people don't want to work that hard, even to improve their own lives. They want someone else to do the work for them and serve it up neatly on a platter. But the truth is, nobody can do the work for us. Only *we* have the power to transform our lives.

The task ahead of you, if it's worth doing at all, is probably long and hard. Most of us have long-term aspirations we're working on, and these require the most commitment of all. The difference between those who succeed and those who fail, is the ability to meet pain head on and not be cowed by it. They're able to "embrace the suck" and still stay the course. Long-term commitment of any kind—to a vocation, a relationship, starting a business—requires an almost endless series of small painful actions. This is the necessary pain we must go through in order to make our dreams a reality. Unnecessary pain, like worry, just keeps us stuck.

The good news is that every time we confront pain head on, we exercise our discomfort muscles. And this is what builds inner strength. With inner strength and courage, we can meet challenges head on. And that is the greatest comfort of all. Success

51

# Up in the Air

CHANGE IS DIFFICULT for most of us. And trying to alter any hardwired habit usually requires a great deal of courage and individual effort. One of my clients who is about to leave his job recently described to me the feeling of quitting as similar to what he felt when he first went skydiving. The idea was something that he had carefully considered and grew excited about for years. Yet when the actual time came for him to jump, staring out into the abyss below, he was gripped with an unimaginable fear of the unknown. The instructor had to literally push him out the door.

Here's the thing though: *all* of life is uncertain—whether we're jumping out of an airplane or not. And as we get older, it becomes even more uncertain. When we are younger, we may assume that if we do all the right things—go to college, get a good job, get married, make good money and so on—we can create a certain future. But ask anyone who has buried a loved one, been downsized or divorced, and they will tell you "not so." It's a cliché to say that we are living in an age of unprecedented anxiety, and if you look around you, it's easy to see why. War in the Middle East, a sputtering economy at home, daily terrorist threats, school shootings, rogue nations with nuclear capability—this is a new age of uncertainty.

Of course, the problem is not so much the uncertainty, but rather our insistence that it should be different. As Americans, we invest an inordinate amount of time and energy in trying to get reality to match our expectations of how things *ought* to be. We strive for a security that we fully believe is attainable, while all the evidence would seem to suggest otherwise. The paradox of striving for external forms of security is that the larger the fortress you build, the more vulnerable you feel to attack. Just as the more stuff you have, the more insurance you need to cover it. But real security—at least the kind worth having—is truly an inside job.

The evidence of this can be seen in a terrific documentary film entitled "Lemonade" which I recently watched. For anyone currently "up in the air" or trying to figure out what to do next, this film is a revelation—and a celebration. The film documents the lives of sixteen former advertising professionals who have recently been let go. What do people who were once paid to be creative for a living do when they're fired? Well, they get inventive with their own lives. One person became the artist that he was always meant to be. A young woman became a yoga instructor and holistic health counselor. Another turned his passion for coffee into a thriving gourmet coffee business. The film is the brainchild of Erik Proulx, himself a former ad man who was given the axe. In order to overcome his own inertia and help others like himself, he started the website www.pleasefeedtheanimals.com. Check it out when you have the time.

If you were to speak to any of these people, I'm sure they would say that the hardest part of beginning any new enterprise is just getting started. The task ahead, if it's worth doing at all, is often long and difficult. Even worse, the outcome is unknown and the fear of failure always present. But if you know anything about static and kinetic energy, you'll also know that it's much harder to get something moving from a dead stop than it is to keep it moving once in motion. As a coach, this is how I see my role. Sometimes I'm the locomotive giving them a push out of the station. Sometimes, I'm the skydiving instructor shoving them out the door! It's doesn't really matter how you get started, so long as you get started.

A couple of years ago when I wanted to learn how to surf, I attended a surf camp in Mexico. It was humbling and frustrating trying to get up on that surfboard for the first time. Just when I was nearly there, a big wave would come along and pummel me, forcing me to swallow half of Sayulita Bay (along with my pride). But I stuck with it. And eventually, after a few days' war of attrition, something clicked and almost effortlessly, I stood up on the board as a wave carried me safely to the shore. The thought of it still makes me smile. At the end of the week, the instructor left us with what I thought was a brilliant piece of advice. "Remember," she said, "the best surfer is the one having the most fun."

Whether you're learning to surf, starting a business, jumping out of a plane or trying to land a new job—the outcome is always uncertain. To be alive is to live with uncertainty every single day. Pain, difficulty, loss, rejection, failure: this is our lot as fragile human beings. But it need not get in the way of what we need to do for ourselves. Remember, the purpose of life is not to live so carefully that you eliminate all the risk—but rather to live it so well that even death, or the fear of it, cannot remove your joy or stand in your way.

# Operating Instructions

NEIL SAT OPPOSITE me in my office. The hollowed-out stare and chewed-to-the-quick fingernails told me this was a man who probably hadn't slept or eaten much in days. As the 29-year-old CEO of a highly successful startup tech firm, he was at his wits end. The company he helped to create was undergoing explosive growth that had caught him by surprise, requiring a new infusion of venture capital, dozens of new hires and a major company restructuring. He missed the good old days, he told me, when it was just him and his partner working from his Brooklyn apartment. "I don't get it," he confessed. "This is what I always wanted. I just wish I knew what the hell I was doing!"

Lots of very successful and accomplished people feel this way some of the time. Or maybe all of the time. They are troubled with high levels of self-doubt and anxiety about their own abilities. Some even believe they are "faking it" and live in terror of actually being "found out." I remember reading an interview with Jodie Foster some years ago. She had been acting in movies since she was nine, and had just won an Oscar for her role in *The Accused*. And yet she couldn't shake the feeling of fraudulence. "I felt like an impostor," she said. "I kept thinking that someday they would find out I didn't know what I was doing. I didn't. And I still don't."

Look, it's okay to not know what you're doing sometimes. We all, to some degree, feel uncertain at work. A lot of our time is spent developing workarounds and elaborate coping mechanisms to pretend that we do in fact, know what we're doing. (Wall Street has developed this to a fine art. Too big to fail? Yeah, right!) Yet most people, if they're honest, will probably tell you it's about fine-tuning your instincts, a good deal of luck and educated guess work. The fact is that we cannot avoid *not* knowing, because life is full of surprises. But what we can do is learn to quiet the impostor that lurks within.

## RELAX

Worry makes you tense and uptight. You make lousy decisions (and a poor impression) when you're nervous. So the very first step is to simply get out of your own way and just breathe. Nothing is that big of a deal. Honestly. Observe anyone doing good work in almost any field of endeavor and what you'll inevitably find is someone in a very relaxed state of body and mind. This is what psychologists sometimes describe as "flow." It is the sweet spot where concentration and control blend effortlessly to produce optimum performance. As true for bricklayers as it is for musicians. We can only do our very best work when we are fully present to the unfolding moment.

## GET THE FACTS

Are you seeing the full picture, or operating with a limited field of vision? You cannot make a good decision without having the facts. It is often said that: "A problem well stated is a problem half solved." One way to do this is to ask a lot of questions. Read. Research. Read some more. Instead of wallowing in the anxiety of not knowing, make it your mission to be as informed on this topic as you can possibly be. Don't even attempt to solve an issue without first collecting all of the facts in an impartial manner.

## ASK FOR ADVICE

If you don't understand something, own up to it, and seek out those who do. It is not a sign of weakness to ask for help when you need it, it is a sign of intelligence. And most people are flattered to be asked for their "expert opinion." Years ago when I was a recruiter, I watched a lot of people interview for jobs they were clearly not qualified for. That's okay, I wasn't necessarily qualified to be interviewing them. But given the choice between two candidates—one who was 100% certain of everything, and another who said something like "I may not know the answer to that, but I know I can find out, and I'm a quick study"—guess who always got the job?

## EXPERIMENT

It hardly matters what you do, as long as you do something. It has been my observation that the most successful people, in life and work, are those who can assemble the facts, and then take swift and decisive action to course correct. They don't stew over problems, and they don't agonize once a decision has been made. They do this by effecting change in the areas they can, and then letting go of the rest. In the words of Goethe: "Boldness has genius, power and magic in it."

It's okay to feel like a phony sometimes. Trust me, you're in good company! Maybe it's even healthy if it spurs us to learn more and make better decisions. Most of us underestimate our true value and strengths. But buried deep under all the self-doubt is the sense that you are I AM infinitely capable. Even in the midst of not knowing sometimes, it is still possible to enjoy peace of mind when we learn to fully trust ourselves.

# CHAPTER FOUR

# Courage

*"Whatever you are meant to do, do it now. The conditions are always impossible."*

—

**Dorothy Lessing**

8/1/19

# Letting Your Guard Down

I NEVER SAW MY father cry. Not at my brother's wedding, our cousin's funeral or my college graduation. It may have been his buttoned-up Teutonic heritage, or former training in the army, but one thing is certain, Dad wasn't very open with his emotions. Whenever I'd ask him about his feelings, his facial muscles would twitch and he'd fob me off with a "better go ask your mother."

Being vulnerable isn't about being weak; it's about finding the necessary courage to let yourself be really seen, warts and all. This can be especially difficult for men like my father, many of whom were trained from a young age to equate any overt displays of emotion with looking weak. The expectations for men tend to center on dominance, control, and avoiding weakness at all costs. "Big boys don't cry." We are frightened that if we reveal too much of our interior landscape that others may exploit it, or think less of us. But paradoxically, it is at our most vulnerable that we are often most powerful.

This week I had a conversation with a client who is struggling to keep his job. Andy, a senior managing director, could easily pass for a twin brother of TV tough guy Tony Soprano. A big burly trader, he is usually a man of few words during our coaching sessions.

But this time, our discussion was altogether different. Feeling stuck and worried about his precarious work situation, his eyes welled up as he shared his recent professional failures with me.

Due to a number of "mistakes" he had made at work over the previous months, the CEO told Andy that his position was in jeopardy. He was put on a "performance improvement plan," which had the opposite of the desired effect. All week long, Andy had been lashing out and blaming others at the office in order to deflect attention from himself, all the while deeply knowing that he is responsible. It wasn't easy for him to admit his feelings of ineptitude to me, and yet, he confided afterwards how cathartic it felt to talk (and cry) it out. Walking around projecting an image of "strength" and "togetherness" was, he said, way more exhausting than his actual job.

Why is it so difficult to let our guard down, to let ourselves be vulnerable? Maybe it's because we have bought into the notion that people only admire us for our strengths. That the only way to win the respect and admiration of our peers is by exhibiting our all-knowing competencies. We set ourselves up as gods to be worshipped, and then wonder why we are unable to connect. But real power, real respect, can never be bought or coerced. The history books are littered with false gods and fallen dictators, brought down by the weight of their own hubris.

What all good leaders eventually come to realize is that true loyalty and respect is about opening yourself up to a conversation where you invite people in—tell them the truth, and find the common ground necessary to do great things together. Keep yourself guarded, and others will respond in kind, which severely hinders the way of progress and limits the possibility of any meaningful connection. One of the challenges for Andy has been having the

*NO*

courage to say, "I don't know" or "what do you think?" Like him, we can strive so hard to appear "in charge," that we actively disinvite open participation and new ideas, surrounding ourselves instead with sycophantic "Yes Men." (The character Michael Scott in *The Office* is the absurdist comedy version of this.)

Good leaders know that when you behave authentically and show respect for those with whom you work, they will usually respond in kind, bringing forward their best ideas and work. Similarly, in the personal realm, power and intimacy are polar opposites. In any relationship, vulnerability is the fuel that propels it forward, and ultimately decides whether or not that relationship will grow. The more we try to make ourselves "powerful"—by projecting confidence and strength—the less likely is the possibility of a genuine connection. No relationship founded solely on power, no matter how well shared, can ever survive the tiny shifts in balance that inevitably occur over time. Real intimacy—the lasting kind—is based on mutual vulnerability.

Letting others into your "emotional space" is about being so open that you become capable of being hurt, though being hurt is not necessarily a guarantee. In fact, most of the time, the opposite is true. Most people are touched by the willingness to share our own vulnerabilities, which in turn gives them permission to reveal themselves also. A couple of months ago, I wrote about the difficulty of my mother's passing in a newsletter I called *Scar Tissue*, and the response to that post blew me away. I was overwhelmed by the flood of support and kind emails I got from friends and strangers alike. That wasn't my intention of course, but it was the result of a shared openness.

Learning to love your weakness as much as you revel in your strength requires great courage. But the potential rewards far outweigh the risk. So go ahead and have that conversation that you've been meaning to have. Invite people in. Nothing is as imprisoning as perfection, and nothing as courageous as the will to truly be yourself.

# Sowing the Seeds of Possibility

WHEN I WAS 6, I won my elementary school science fair by attempting to grow bean sprouts out of an empty milk carton. Hardly groundbreaking stuff, but it sure was fun. Interestingly, my experiment was not a success. Sadly, nothing sprouted. I suspect now that I was awarded first prize because the judges could see my crushing disappointment, and noticed from my copious notes that I had tried really hard to do it all by myself (unlike some of the other fancier projects that had parents' fingerprints all over them).

Science fairs are designed to encourage you to think critically and to risk failure. You put forward a hypothesis, and then develop a rigorous set of tests to support it. The thesis does not even have to be correct, therefore there can be no failure. During that fair, I learned to take immense pride in my little bean sprout experiment, and I also learned how to speak effectively in front of a group of people. Not a bad return on investment!

Part of what I do now as a coach is to encourage people to sow the seeds of possibility. Not to be afraid of messing up. As adults, we are programmed to fear failure above all else. Failure stings; failure hurts; it makes us feel bad. Yet, the whole history of scientific progress is littered with people being wrong before they were right.

Without it, there would be no penicillin, no smallpox vaccine, no electric light bulb. Gregor Mendel, Louis Pasteur and Thomas Edison were all massive "failures" in their day. *No EPIC life-kids*

I often work with executives who want to move forward but are feeling stuck. They ask me: How do I connect to others in the industry, develop the absolute best business plan or create the ideal pitch to achieve my goals? And my response is: Who says it needs to be perfect? Isn't all of life, in the end, a grand experiment of some sort?

The problem with most of us is that we are afraid to get it wrong. We are too busy trying to formulate a compelling strategy or flawless opening line. And then the opportunity is past.

Is there someone you've been meaning to call recently? Then *Crystal* pick up the phone. Some idea that sounds crazy, but simply won't let you go? Give it a shot. What have you got to lose? Sure, you may need to do your homework, but too often I get pushback from my clients: "You want me to do *what*? But that'll never work!" And I say, "Really? Have you actually tried? Have you really tried to do something in a different way, or are you just afraid of looking foolish?"

In 2004, Wangari Maathai was awarded the Nobel Peace Prize for her humanitarian work in reforesting her native Kenya. Returning to her land after several years teaching in Nairobi, she was shocked and dismayed to find the once fertile forest of her youth stripped of its natural cover to make way for coffee and tea plantations. Villagers now had to walk miles just to get firewood, and the chemical run-off from the pesticides was poisoning their water supply. She decided that one obvious solution to their problem was to simply plant more trees.

She organized a small group of determined women to help her. Their initial goal was to plant seven trees, which they did. Five of those died immediately. Pretty discouraging, by anyone's standards.

But they didn't stop there. Instead they learned from their many mistakes and became highly adept at planting. Other neighbors watched what they were doing and eventually the entire community got involved. The simple idea spread, and soon they were able to restore vast tracts of Kenyan farmland.

What difference does one tree make? A lot, as it turns out. Today, The Greenbelt Movement has harvested more than 40 million trees across the African continent. Acres of indigenous forest have been restored and protected, and thousands of women and their families are standing up for their rights and those of their communities- living healthier, more productive lives. Imagine if she had given up after the first few trees had failed?

We all suffer on occasion from the "gotta get it right" syndrome. Leaders especially, feel a lot of internal pressure to be in charge, to always know the exact right thing to do next. Talk about stress. But if you're not at least okay with being wrong, then it's unlikely you will ever come up with anything original. When the old roadmaps don't serve you anymore, it's time to join the rest of us and simply make it up as you go along. Plant a few seeds and see which ones may sprout.

The beauty of thinking in this way is that it releases us from the tyranny of failure, and frees us up to try new ways of doing things. Wangari Maathai didn't know she would start a movement just by planting a few trees, and she certainly didn't know she'd win the Nobel Peace Prize. She just took that first next step, and then the next, and then the next.

And you can too.

# Little Feat

$\text{I}$N NOVEMBER OF 2014, I gave birth to a new venture: a bouncing baby boy named James. He's pretty cute if I say so myself, and has so drastically altered my universe that it's hard to even remember what life was like before he was born. Of course, there is the love that you feel (bursting and unconditional), coupled with the fear that this engenders (what if something happens to him?). And then there is the fatigue (chronic and unending), that can make you look and act like a crazy person.

As an older first-time parent, I knew it wouldn't be easy, but nor did I imagine it would be this hard. Going to work is a doddle compared to the challenge of raising a child. Now that I've managed to survive the first 3 months, I thought I would share some of the learning that may have broader application beyond the newborn phase.

## YOU THINK YOU'RE IN CHARGE. THAT'S SO CUTE!

My husband was an absolute trooper. Together, we read all the books, did the classes, hospital tours, endless rounds of doctor visits. We learned how to hold, swaddle and soothe a crying infant (much easier when they're made of plastic!). We even took a class on "hypnobirthing," that through the magic of mind control, promised us a calm, pain-free and "natural" birthing experience. But once we arrived at the hospital, that magical Unicorn quickly disappeared, replaced by modern medicine: induction, twenty-six hours of labor, followed by emergency C-section. In the end, I was grateful just to make it out of there alive. A healthy baby was an added bonus. You think you're in control—until you're not.

## DON'T LISTEN TO THE ODDS

Being of "advanced maternal age," I was told that the odds of having a completely healthy baby were stacked heavily against me. At 41, it seemed foolhardy, dangerous even. Had I listened to the "March of Dimes" guidelines, I would never have even tried. But deep down in my soul I knew that I wanted to be a mother, and all the scaremongering statistics would not deter me from that. I didn't know if I could, I just knew that I had to try. We all have our deep desire, our impossible dream. If it's in you, don't deny it. And for heaven's sake, do not listen to "the odds." They are an abstraction. Trust your intuition. Then trust it some more.

## GO SKIN TO SKIN

When we first took our little boy home, he was totally inconsolable. That first night was the absolute worst. He wailed like Janis Joplin, and would not stop. Then my husband remembered something they did in the hospital—skin to skin. The baby was plopped, naked and howling, onto my chest and it calmed him right down. He even slept for an hour or two. Overwhelmed by this unfamiliar world, he just needed to know we were close, and would protect him. There is no substitute for skin to skin contact in baby world. Or face to face connection in the real world. It says, "I'm here. I see you. I'm listening." There is no electronic device that can do that for you.

## WAIT AND SEE

Like a lot of first-time parents, we tried to be as "ready" as possible, buying ahead of time all the things we thought we would need. The trouble is, you don't know what you're going to need or if any of it will even work. We of course bought the wrong formula, and within two weeks, he had outgrown all of the newborn clothes and diapers. Far better to wait and see what you're going to need, before actually buying anything. This applies to other investments as well. You may *think* you really need it, but chances are you probably don't.

## SOMETIMES THE THING YOU DON'T WANT IS EXACTLY WHAT YOU NEED

Parenting in the early stages can feel a lot like being a shift worker in a factory: endless repetition of mundane tasks, until you don't know who you are anymore. Feed, burp, sway, swaddle, wash. Now rinse and repeat. Infants are the drill sergeants of parenting boot camp, and if you let them, they will break you. Sometimes, I'd be so spent that the thought of even going outside would exhaust me. "No thanks, I'm good!" I couldn't see that I needed saving—from myself. So welcome the friend or partner who says to you, "C'mon, you're coming with me." If someone says to you, "You look like you could use a break. Let's go grab a coffee," take the offer and for heaven's sake, go! Get outside. Sometimes a simple change of scenery may be just what you need to regain your composure.

## THERE IS NEVER A GOOD TIME

There is never a good time to have kids, make a big decision or begin something new. The conditions will always be less than ideal. One thing this has done is increase my understanding of, and empathy for my own parents, and indeed all parents who somehow manage to cobble together a life that includes time for work, rest and play. It is the ultimate pay-it-forward endeavor—a lifetime of compromise and sacrifice for which you may or may not get thanks.

In the words of Dorothy Lessing: "Whatever you are meant to do, do it now. The conditions are always impossible."

# Rewriting Your Story

Gina slumped into the chair in my office and unloaded all the things that were bothering her—things she wanted us to work on. It was not a short list either. Her boss had overlooked her for promotion several times. At 45, she felt there was an age bias toward younger employees in the company that she had been with for 15 years. She was, she told me, "too old" to go back for an MBA. New neighbors had recently moved into the apartment above hers and every night sounded like they were rehearsing for *Riverdance*. On top of all this, the dating pool for a single over 40 year-old woman in Manhattan was slim. All the good men were either married, gay, or only interested in 20 year-old hotties.

The breezy manner in which this was delivered suggested a degree of familiarity with the story from previous telling and re-telling, almost a gleeful relishing of the unfortunate details that she wore proudly like a badge of honor. Finally, after 50 minutes I asked simply: "Gina, do you feel like you're in charge of your life?" She looked at me quizzically, as though I hadn't been listening. "Well, obviously not," she shot back. "Or I wouldn't be here talking to you."

## STORY FONDLING

Children often enjoy hearing the same stories, or watching the same movies over and over again—because there is great comfort in knowing the outcome. Familiar stories help us to organize a frightening world into a comprehensible framework. Stories make sense. Stories create order out of chaos.

As adults, we are equally adept at revisiting old story patterns. In coaching parlance, the term we sometimes use for this is "story fondling". The word fondling implies a loving embrace, or a warm caress. The problem with many of our stories is that they are not loving, and very often built around a faulty premise. Sentences that begin with "I've always been a...Everyone in our family is...I've never been really good at...My whole entire life..." may indicate that a story is being told. Sure, it may be comforting and familiar, perhaps even funny, but it is also severely limiting. Stories told often enough become self-fulfilling prophecies. *NO! Stop the stories*

## WHAT'S YOUR STORY?

We all have them. I'm a product of divorce. All my relationships end in tears. I don't like change. I'm not really good with people. The details and how we spin them into a narrative largely determine how we see our lives, and consequently—our experience of living. Whether it's a painful family drama, a tragedy or a comedic farce—the choice is all in how we frame it. The very first step in reclaiming your power is recognizing that everything in your life—how you feel, how you react, how you live, where you work—is a choice. I'm not suggesting that people actively choose illness, or poverty or disability. Of course they don't. But more important than the actual circumstance of your life, is the *story* that you are telling yourself about it. If the story is not serving you, then maybe it's time to try another one? STORY

As a coach, I am privy to a lot of peoples' stories. It's often tempting to want to "fix" their circumstances rather than examining their imprisoning beliefs. Don't think your thoughts are holding you back? Try this: No one will hire me because I'm too old. I'll never find love. This is not the life I imagined for myself starting out. I thought once I made partner, I would feel different. Everybody's moved on but me, I think I may have missed my chance.

## NEVER TOO LATE

Whatever your particular story, it is vitally important that you remain an active protagonist rather than a hapless victim of circumstance. (Hence my question to Gina: Do you feel you are in charge of your life?) You want to be the kind of hero who doesn't listen to naysayers and enjoys beating the odds. And it's never too late to begin. For every Mark Zuckerberg who gets off to an early start, there are thousands of others who do remarkable things well into their middle and twilight years. YES! ME!

Julia Child didn't learn to cook until she was 40. Didn't launch her masterpiece cookbook till she was nearly fifty. Frank McCourt worked all his life as a teacher in New York City's public schools. He was 66 when he published his memoir Angela's Ashes. If ever there was an example of reframing a story, this is it. He took what should have been a devastating childhood, and with honesty and humor, spun it into pure narrative gold—and the Pulitzer Prize.

At this years' Academy Awards, you may have seen David Seidler, the 73-year-old former stutterer winning his first Oscar for writing *The King's Speech*. Or how about Kimani Maruge, who had to wait 80 years for the right to go to school. When free primary education was finally introduced in his native Kenya, Maruge knew it was his last chance to learn how to read and write. At the ripe old age of 84, he enrolled in the first grade at his local school. In 2005, Maruge addressed the United Nations in New York on the importance of free primary education. This year will see the release of a new movie about his life, entitled *The First Grader*.

If the life you are living is smaller than the one you once imagined, take a good look at how you are telling your story—to yourself, to your spouse, to the world at large. Make sure the narrative is serving you, and not the other way around. In a world of infinite freedom and choice, it is never too late to rewrite your story.

The past is prologue. The rest is still unwritten.

# Making Friends With Terror
## (The Art of Public Speaking)

T HERE'S AN OLD joke told by Jerry Seinfeld which goes something like this: "According to most studies, people's number one fear is public speaking. Number two is death. Wait a minute, death is number *two*? This means that to the average person, if you go to a funeral, you're better off in the casket than doing the eulogy!"

Ever since reading about The TAI Group here in New York, I've been longing to take one of their courses in public speaking. Two months ago, I finally had that opportunity. The course I took is their popular 2-day foundation course, titled "Communicating With Power and Presence."

Truth be told, I'd already had some training. Unfortunately, most of it was in grammar school when I managed to maintain a strong presence on the Forensics Team. Since that time, speaking as a part of my job has forced me to confront some of my own issues. When called on to present, I sometimes find myself searching for excuses. But since one of my coaching values is to "stretch"—to get beyond the comfort zone—I knew the time had come for me to really tackle this head on.

Drawing upon roots in theater, psychology and leadership development, TAI teaches people how to properly engage an audience.

Without an engaged audience, you are literally talking to yourself. First, let me say how much I enjoyed this workshop. It was challenging, experiential, humbling, and of course...absolutely brilliant. For anyone who presents on a regular basis, this course should be mandatory. Hell, even if you never need to present, this would still be worth the price of admission.

Gifford Booth, director and co-founder of TAI, taught the class along with coach-in-training, Michael Filan. Both gentlemen were friendly and inviting. One of the things I loved was the democracy of the "workshop" format. There was no regard given to anyone's title or rank. Most in attendance were senior or C-level people, but in this little windowless room for two whole days, we were just nine people wanting to learn how to communicate more effectively. I came away with a whole arsenal of tools, some of which are worth sharing here.

## CHARACTER IS KING

The conventional wisdom holds that "content is king" when it comes to presentation. But according to TAI, this is only a small part of it. In their world, the essence of a great presentation involves:

Character – 55%

Craft – 38%

Content – 7%

Yes, good content is necessary, but it is not sufficient. This means that we should step out from behind PowerPoint and give the audience a little piece of ourselves—and our personality. When I first stood up in front of the group—under bright stage lights, feeling nervous—I was concerned that my message wasn't useful and that I didn't have the chops. I was terrified that they would hear every mistake or "um" that I'd say. Instead, what I came to learn from Gifford was that I was a natural communicator. A "natural"? Yep.

Once I allowed my authentic self to come through, I actually had a gift as a presenter. The same skills that make me a good "private" one-on-one speaker during my coaching sessions are the ones that enable me to be a good public speaker: good eye-contact, listening, gesturing, and animated facial expressions. The goal is not to "give a speech" (like I used to back in the 7th grade), but rather to make your presentation a "conversation"—even though the audience is not talking. When I did this, I noticed my credibility and presence increase.

## TELL ME A STORY

Since our early ancestors first gathered around the campfire, people have been hardwired to respond to story. The response to shared human experience is deep-seated within all of us, and we'd be foolish not to use it in our presentations. Think you're not a storyteller? Nonsense! We all do it naturally in our day-to-day life all the time: "You won't believe what happened to me today..." "Are you sitting down? Cause I am gonna tell you something that is going to rock your world..." Companies, governments, advertisers, and good speakers all understand the inherent power of narrative. Telling a story is the surest way to hook a listener's imagination, and, once you have their attention, get your message across. The great success of the Obama election campaign was due in no small part to the power of his "narrative." His personal story combined with his sweeping message of "change" galvanized his followers and secured his election over John McCain.

## WAIT FOR IT TO LAND

When you're out in front of a crowd, time seems to move very slowly. What feels like an eternity to you, may in fact, be only a half second to your audience. The tendency for most people is to hurry, rushing headlong to get to the end. Throughout the workshop, we were encouraged to slow down, giving our words a moment to "land." Look people in the eye, give them a chance to acknowledge and respond to what you are actually saying, just like you would in a real conversation. In practice, this is really hard to do. Most people tend to just glance furtively at an audience without really connecting. All good speakers understand the power of looking at their audience, pausing for effect, leaving space so that their words have room to be heard.

## CONNECT WITH ONE PERSON AT A TIME

Great politicians understand that connecting on an individual level is key. Probably the greatest example in modern history is Bill Clinton. Like him or not, the man was a masterful "connector." If he was speaking in a town hall setting and someone asked a question, he would speak directly to that person as if they were the only one in the room. You would think that other people might feel left out, but in fact, the opposite is true. Whenever a speaker is connecting with someone in the audience, we unconsciously "lean in" to observe what is going on. The same phenomenon known as "rubbernecking"—which causes the highway to be backed up for miles—can actually help you as a presenter, if you know how to use it. What people call "magnetism" is really the ability to fully engage one person so that they feel special.

# BREATHE

Coach Mike was especially good at reminding us of our breathing, or lack thereof. While standing in front of the audience, Mike told us to scan our bodies for tension, to feel our feet on the floor and to take a minute to see the audience. He showed us how to take deep breaths that result from diaphragm movement. During this exercise we let air in slowly for five counts, then we held the breath for 5 counts, and then slowly let the air out for five counts and repeated when necessary. Neglect of proper breathing technique results in fast, breathless speech and plain old discomfort on the part of the speaker. After a while, I could spot when a speaker was not breathing properly during their talk because my own breath often mirrored theirs. According to Gifford, "the difference between fear and excitement…is breathing."

# PRACTICE

How do you get to Carnegie Hall? Practice. In Malcolm Gladwell's book, *Outliers*, he mentions the "10,000-hour Rule," claiming that the key to success in any field is, to a large extent, a matter of practicing a specific task for a total of around 10,000 hours. Since we are not born with public speaking skills, we need to practice in order to see results. For me, this means prepping for hours before I deliver a presentation and, over time, increasing the number of talks I give. A great leader is able to exert influence because he or she knows their craft. You need to be so familiar with your content that you can easily go "off message" and still find your way back into the presentation without missing a beat. How do you do that? Know your material.

## IT'S NOT ABOUT YOU

After I had finished my piece, Gifford instructed each of the participants to share what they saw and felt as they listened to me. What astonished me most was that the audience found pieces of my story to be compelling for entirely different reasons. What each person heard was unique to their individual lens, just as two people can read the same book and have an entirely different experience. I thought I had control over listener takeaway, but I didn't. Nobody does. When it comes to speaking, power and control are polar opposites. On the other hand, power and vulnerability go hand in hand. If you have the courage to reveal your true character in front of an audience, your message will resonate.

All the audience really wants is a well-prepared, honest speaker who believes in her message and is willing to passionately communicate that belief. So give up the need to "control" the audience. Because ultimately, it's not even about you—it's about them.

# Painting with Scissors

THE YEARS AFTER World War II were not kind to the artist Henri Matisse. The war had cost him his home, his marriage and in a particularly cruel twist of fate—a serious illness had robbed him of his ability to stand or paint. Immobile and unable to work, he became depressed and bedbound. To get out of this downward spiral, he knew he had to find a way to work again. And so, using only a scissors and some colored paper, he began by cutting out some crude shapes and pinning them loosely together to make collage compositions. This desire to create, coupled with a doggedness of will would result in some of his best-loved and most enduring work. The whimsical "Cut-Out" series, almost childlike in their simplicity, were the subject of a recent retrospective at the MOMA in New York that celebrates Matisse's life and work.

## TURNING WEAKNESS INTO STRENGTH

For Matisse, it was his growing infirmity and failing eyesight that opened up the door to a new world of creative possibility. For Brian Grazer, it was a lifelong learning difficulty that he believes helped to equip him with the necessary skills to become a successful movie producer in Hollywood. Like a lot of dyslexics, Grazer had serious trouble in school. It was a difficult and anxious time for him. This led to him developing a whole host of compensatory skills: rote memory learning of large chunks of text, immaculate preparation before all tests and meetings, acute listening skills, the ability to negotiate with teachers for a passing grade. Skills that would later serve him very well as one of the most prolific and successful movie producers of all time.

While dyslexia is certainly a disability, it obviously does not determine anyone's future. According to some recent studies, as many as 30% of all successful entrepreneurs have some form of dyslexia. Notables include Virgin founder Richard Branson, financial guru Charles Schwab and David Neeleman, founder of Jetblue Airways. Why is this? Well, it could be that dyslexics are less risk averse than the general population, allowing them to see opportunities where others do not. According to Grazer, his dyslexia had allowed him to become "comfortable with failure" early on, and this had a freeing effect on him. It could also be that in identifying their greatest weakness, they are more apt to leverage other strengths. They succeed not in spite of their disability, but *because* of it.

## WHAT IS YOUR GREATEST WEAKNESS?

Nearly every job interviewer asks some version of this question, and it might be worth asking yourself now and again. Because contained in every "weakness" is often a clue to a corresponding strength, waiting to be developed. Inherent in any ending, is often the thread of a new beginning waiting to be found. So a business venture fails—maybe it was the wrong business to begin with? And maybe now is the time to move swiftly and early to the next big idea. So a relationship ends—maybe now you are free to reclaim your sense of self, and finally discover who you really are? This is not magical "positive thinking" (though there's nothing wrong with that), but learning to recognize the seed of possibility in even our weakest spot.

Consider Albert Maysles (1926-2015), widely regarded as one of the greatest documentary filmmakers of his generation. Together with his brother David, he took on a range of subjects from Muhammad Ali to the Rolling Stones, creating in the process a new "verité" style of cinema that is still widely in use today. But for the first 20 years of his life, young Albert rarely spoke. He was laughed at, ridiculed, widely assumed to be stupid. Naturally, his parents were worried and sent him to see therapist after therapist. But he wasn't dumb or even shy; he had an undiagnosed learning disability. He rarely spoke because he was so intent upon listening, afraid that he was missing things. But once he took up a film camera, the world finally made sense to him. His job now was to watch and listen, and he excelled at it.

## LEVERAGE YOUR STRENGTHS

Most of us work hard to improve or eliminate our perceived areas of weakness. Some are even sent to see me by their bosses, with the unspoken hope that I can somehow "fix" them. But my own experience, as a coach and as a consultant, tells me that it's very hard to change anyone who does not want to be changed. Far better, to find out what that person does well, and try to find ways to properly leverage it. Similarly, when it comes to our own relationships, it can be very easy to point out all the flaws in others, highlighting their weaknesses. But we all do better—as people, as parents, as companies—when we are encouraged to play to our strengths.

We all work with certain limitations. There is rarely enough time, money or resources to accomplish all that we would like. But maybe there is something you can do within those limitations? Constraints can often be good, forcing us to choose what is essential and come up with creative solutions where others have failed. In the words of Teddy Roosevelt: "Do what you can, with what you have, where you are." Matisse found a way to make art by painting with scissors. What can you do?

# CHAPTER FIVE

# Freedom of Mind

*"No one can make you feel inferior without your consent."*

—

Eleanor Roosevelt

# Cool Running

IF YOU HAVEN'T seen the movie "42"—I highly recommend that you do. It is the inspirational true story of how Jackie Robinson broke through Major League Baseball's color barrier during the 1950's. One of the most powerful scenes in the movie has Robinson trying to concentrate at bat, while in the background, he is taunted mercilessly, relentlessly, by a snarling southern bigot. It takes an almost superhuman effort of will for him not to respond in the moment. And in the next scene, we see the toll on his psyche of this impossible task. It is compelling drama, and utterly devastating to watch.

Thankfully, most of us will never experience first-hand this extreme kind of provocation. But every day, the opportunity is there for us to get our chains yanked in ways that are not helpful. If you live in New York City, those opportunities multiply just by walking down the street. Most people are not even aware that their buttons are being pushed, causing them to react from "old programming" well below the conscious level. Which is why we get angry meltdowns on TV, public outbursts on the subway, tossed salads and computers at work (I've seen both).

Whenever you are triggered, you are reacting emotionally. And very often, what you're reacting to is not the incident itself, but something else entirely. It may be something that happened weeks, months or even years before. And it doesn't always have to be a great trauma either. It might just be a time when you felt small, weak, stupid, ignored, excluded or abandoned. And getting your button pushed in this way takes you right back to that unpleasant feeling, causing you to lash out. But if you work with other people (and most of us do), then we need to learn coping mechanisms to help us "run cool." With some awareness, and a little practice, you can learn to do this.

## KNOW YOUR TRIGGERS

If something has bothered you in the past, chances are it's going to bother you in the future, unless you can learn to process it differently. Take a look at what are some of the "hot button" issues for you. Write them down if necessary. We all have them, and what might make you see red may not even register as yellow for someone else. Telltale signs you're about to get triggered include rapid heartbeat, shortness of breath, stiff neck, a sudden urge to hit something (or someone). This is the time to choose your words and actions *very* carefully. The first step in defusing any potential land mines is in knowing where exactly they lie, and what they look like.

## TIME OUT

The goal, insofar as it's possible, should always be to create a "gap" between stimulus and response. As mature individuals, we always want to evaluate carefully any incoming—and then respond appropriately. The ways to do this are many. Saving your heated email response to your draft folder is a big one. Never write an

*I 'M AN ACTOR*

angry or emotional email, without letting it first sit overnight. Take a walk. Get out of the room. There are verbal stalling tactics too: "That's interesting, tell me more about that?" You always want to be an Actor, not a Reactor. Only *you* decide how you will act, not somebody else. Even when someone is rude or insulting, you still have the power to choose your reaction. "Oh, that's interesting," you might say. "I wonder why he's so enraged?"

## REHEARSE FOR SUCCESS

Knowing what is likely to set you off, it is possible to *rehearse*, yes rehearse, an appropriate response to this situation. This is the secret of all skilled political operatives: talking points. They talk about what they want to talk about, regardless of the question. No matter how enticing, they simply refuse point blank to take the bait. And that takes some real practice. It can be invaluable to rehearse how you might handle a tricky question or situation. By doing so, you take all of the heat out of a hot-button issue, and respond to it coolly, even in the face of aggressive or deliberate provocation. No person (or thing) can cause you to react a certain way, because you've already chosen your response.

## LEARN THE LANGUAGE

At the root of all misunderstanding are unexpressed needs, wants and desires. Most of the things that we say are bothering us, are not what is really bothering us. We just get them confused. One of the training models I use in coaching is called NVC (Nonviolent communication), often referred to as "compassionate" communication. Its goal is to foster consciousness and understanding through the careful use of highly specific language. It's a useful tool, and if everyone could use it, there would be no need for coaches like me.

The *inability* to express what we are truly feeling can have heartbreaking consequences. NVC reminds us of the enormous power that words carry, and how to use them wisely. The true legacy of Jackie Robinson extends well beyond the baseball field. He showed, as Thomas Jefferson once said how, "one man with courage makes a majority." With his courage, self-discipline, and superb baseball skills, Jackie Robinson changed the world by small increments, paving the way for Martin Luther King and other proponents of non-violence who would follow in his wake.

Nobody, but nobody, could push his buttons—not without his consent.

# Breaking Bad

$B$ACK IN 2004, a U.S. marine in Iraq was given the unenviable task of figuring out what was igniting the recent spate of riots inside the city of Kufa, located 90 miles north of Baghdad. After closely studying videotapes of previous riots, he began to see a pattern. People would gather in the plaza to protest. Over the next few hours, their numbers would gradually swell. Then the food vendors would appear, followed by spectators eager to watch the drama unfold. Angry slogans were chanted until finally, somebody would throw a rock at the police, and then all hell would break loose.

When the American soldier met with the Mayor of Kufa to discuss peacekeeping solutions, he made one odd request. Would it be possible, he asked, to keep the food vendors out of the plaza? The mayor agreed. A few weeks later, another crowd gathered near the great mosque of Kufa. The police stood nervously by, awaiting trouble. By dusk, the crowd was growing hungry and restless. But when the kebab sellers failed to appear, the protesters became dispirited. One by one, they all drifted home to eat. By 8pm, the plaza was empty.

The brilliance of this solution was that it required no police intervention at all. Everyone (including angry protesters) needs to eat!

Just one small change in a well-worn routine was enough to alter the outcome. This is one of the many fascinating tales illuminating Charles Duhigg's new book, *The Power of Habit: Why We Do What We Do in Life and Business.* get

Drawing upon research in medicine, neurology and applied psychology, the author shows how habit governs most of our behavior. His central argument is that habits—even the most deeply ingrained ones—can be changed, *if* we understand how they work.

As someone who advises on organizational change, this message struck a deep chord with me. According to Duhigg, about 40% of our actions are not even conscious, they're simply habit. A habit begins when we are prompted by some cue, followed by a routine that brings about a reward. When this cycle of cue-routine-reward gets repeated often enough, it becomes ingrained as "habit." And our brains are very good at creating them. Why? Because routine response requires less mental energy, and our brains are biologically programmed to conserve energy. This can work both for us, and against us.

Witness any top athlete in his "zone" and what you will often see are a series of well-rehearsed behaviors designed to enhance their overall performance. On the flip side, observe any unhappily married couple and what you will often see are negative "habit loops" at work. She talks too much during dinner and as a result he shuts down. She blames him for being "anti-social" causing him to resent her for talking down to him. And on it goes.

## SO HOW DO WE CHANGE BAD HABITS?

First, we need to become *aware* of our triggers. Then we need to work consciously to interrupt the habit loop. Alcoholics Anonymous has done this successfully for years by providing a practical framework for attacking the cues that surround alcohol abuse. While AA uses "twelve steps"—there are, according to Duhigg, 3 major steps involved in breaking any bad habit.

1. **Recognize the cues that trigger certain behaviors.** For a Shopper/smoker, it might be recognizing the feelings of boredom or anxiety that trigger a desire for a cigarette. For an alcoholic, it might be recognizing feelings of loss or loneliness, and the desire to escape those feelings. The same holds true for comfort eating, gambling or any other destructive form of behavior. Understanding the cues is the first step to breaking bad habits.

2. **Interrupt the habit loop.** According to Duhigg, you cannot simply *eradicate* a bad habit. Rather, you must substitute a *new* behavior for the old. For example, let's say you find yourself automatically snacking at 11am every day to relieve boredom. Instead, you might substitute an apple and a vigorous ten-minute walk with a friend. When confronted with the urge to drink, an alcoholic might call his sponsor, or go to a meeting. A smoker might chew a stick of celery. Same cue, different response.

3. **Believe that change is possible.** For any habit to stay changed, people must *believe* that change is actually possible. For a losing football team to win, they must first believe that they can win. A smoker must believe that it is possible for him to be an ex-smoker. This is one of the chief benefits of groups like AA, Weight Watchers and others. If the belief in yourself is weak, you can always tap into the collective belief of a group struggling with similar issues. You say to yourself, "if she can do it, I can do it."

But it's not just individual lives that can benefit when our habits shift. It's also organizations. Even the most dysfunctional companies can transform themselves, *if* the desire for change is there. That's not to say that change is easy or simple. It's not. Real change —the lasting kind—requires genuine courage, lasting commitment, work and the support of others. What Duhigg reminds us however, is that our habits are not destiny. By consciously adjusting our habits to better serve us, we ultimately have the power to transform our lives, our families, our businesses and our communities. And that's a habit worth remembering.

# Shadowboxing

GROWING UP, MY father worked two jobs to support his growing family. It was unglamorous work, the kind that requires sturdy boots year round and insulated overalls during freezing winter months. After work, he liked to unwind with a couple of beers while he sloughed off the day. As a child, I was sometimes fascinated to witness him engaged in full on dialogues…with *himself.* There were whispered asides, gesticulations, finger pointing, head nodding, as I imagine he worked out whatever psychic frustrations bedeviled him. Maybe a client had stiffed him on a job. Maybe some worker had given him lip, or disrespected him. Somebody cut him off in traffic. And here, in the safety of his own home, he could finally give them all a piece of his mind.

Author Terry Real has a name for this: he calls it "shadowboxing." It's when you're boxing with someone who is no longer there, or maybe was never there to begin with. The shadow can be anyone, or anything. Maybe it's your old boss, a parent long gone, a painful incident from childhood, or in the case of my father, maybe the general sense of powerlessness he felt in his job. The trouble with this kind of boxing is that A) It's totally exhausting and B) you can never really "win" because the opponent has long since left the building. By this time, they are no longer even real people, but rather invisible caricatures of those people: ghosts cobbled together from past experience and memory.

We're seeing a lot of shadowboxing in the news these days. While certainly not new, the caricature and demonization of those with opposing viewpoints has reached a new and alarming level of vitriol. Terry Real would argue that we are not really fighting with each other, but rather with the other's "core negative image," which is to say: the *worst* imaginable version of that person. A caricature. Certain of our moral superiority, we focus on all the ways that we are RIGHT and they are wrong. We amplify those qualities and attributes that we find most offensive in the other, and use these as license to discredit, dislike, and even delegitimize.

## US AND THEM

In my work as an executive coach, I will often gather and present written 360 feedback on business leaders at all levels. For people on the receiving end, it can be very difficult to not react negatively or defensively. They may even resort to name calling, which feels good in the moment, but only serves to create more distance and misunderstanding. I encourage my clients to counter this natural instinct by remaining open and curious. Curiosity invites dialogue, which can lead to some useful new insights. I ask them to be *compassionate* with themselves and with those offering the feedback. Both require taking risks.

Effective leadership demands that we avoid shutting down, drawing up the battle lines between Us and Them. Another key foundation of great leadership is the ability to recognize and check our own bias. In order not to demonize the "other", in order not to *weaponize* our contempt, we need to keep a close check on our own worst instinct which is to point the finger of blame. Do not Do

It is a universal truth that what we criticize most harshly in others is often the thing we like least about ourselves. What I hate most about you, may be the very thing I hate most about myself.

In her excellent TED talk entitled "Take the Other to Lunch," Elizabeth Lesser offers these three important tips for navigating a conversation with someone whose viewpoint is fundamentally the opposite of yours.

1. **Don't persuade, defend, or interrupt.**
2. **Be curious, be conversational, be real.**
3. **Listen.**

Perhaps easier said than done, but we could all afford to LISTEN better to what the other side is saying. All great religious and political leaders from history share in common this unique ability: they strive first to understand the other's problem, before seeking out the common ground. They are (or have trained themselves to be) intensely interested in the viewpoints, ideas, and critiques of their peers.

Of course, we can't all be Nelson Mandela, but maybe we can try to understand the "other" point of view without resorting to questioning their intellect or moral integrity. I think the biggest enemy of people who want to make the world a better place is not liberalism or conservatism, it's actually cynicism. Our own cynicism that says nothing will ever change and the world is going to hell in a hand basket. I think that's the *real* enemy, and the one we must guard against.

It may sound very "Kumbaya," but I sincerely believe that deep down we all want the same thing: a feeling of connectedness with others, to live with hope, peace and security. We just have different ideas about how this can be achieved. Shadowboxing an ugly caricature will not help. As the old saying goes, "If you want to change the world, try starting with yourself."

# "No" is a Complete Sentence

ONE OF MY clients recently confessed to me that he told a distant cousin who was visiting from out of town, that he had plans to be in Alaska while she was around. A little "white lie" in order to avoid the obligatory "Hey, we should get together and have dinner." Instead of just coming clean and sharing the simple truth (that he was too busy and didn't feel like meeting up), he created this rather elaborately drawn fiction, worthy of a Seinfeld episode.

If you have trouble saying "no," you're certainly not alone. Last week, I had to say "no" to serving on yet another committee, and it was difficult for me to do because it's a cause that I firmly believe in. But the sense of personal liberation I felt afterwards told me it was the right decision for me. In the past, I might have said yes for fear of hurting people's feelings, or being seen as disagreeable. I was raised, like a lot of girls, to be a people pleaser. So learning to say "no" has been a challenge for me, a learned skill.

A few years ago, I enlisted in an assertiveness training program to sharpen my own skills in this area. Knowing how and when to communicate our thoughts and needs was the focus of the class. I learned that my dislike of saying "no" was deeply embedded in my psyche. But it was also costing me dearly in my work and in my relationships. It was particularly frustrating since I realized I was doing this to myself. With a little practice and some good instruction, I soon learned that saying "no" doesn't have to mean being rude or disagreeable.

## SAYING "NO" RESPECTFULLY

Now, if I want to say "no" to someone who asks me for something, I make a point of saying (if it's true, of course) how much I WANT to support them and why it doesn't work for me. E.G: *"Thank you so much for thinking of me, but I can't commit to this as I have other priorities at the moment..." "No, I'm not available. Is there something we can do so that we can meet halfway?" "No, I don't have the capacity. I have a long-standing appointment for this evening that I need to keep..." "I'm sorry, but now is not a good time for me as I'm in the middle of something else. Maybe we can reconnect at another time?" "I am not the best person to help you with this, maybe you should try X..." "No, I'm not comfortable doing that." "No, I'm not interested." "No."*

For people who don't respect your "no" (and there will be some), my best piece of advice is to simply repeat, calmly and clearly, your stated position (AKA the broken record technique). *"Thank you for thinking of me, but I'm going to have to pass on this. I'd rather say 'no' now than 'I'm sorry' later."*

Why is assertive communication difficult for so many? For starters, it's not something that we're ever taught in school, and we often learn poor communication techniques from those we observed (who also received no formal training). Yet, assertiveness is an essential skill if we are to deal with the world in a mature and responsible fashion.

The right to say "no" without feeling guilty was one of the many "personal" rights I learned I had. Others include:

- The right to say "I don't know" or "I don't understand."
- The right to be treated with dignity and respect.
- The right to decide what is best for me.
- The right to be listened to and taken seriously.
- The right to change my mind.
- The right to make mistakes.

## OPENNESS TO HEARING "NO"

The corollary of this means that we must also be okay when someone says "no" to us. Recently, I had the experience of requesting a meeting with an author whose work I admired. We had met before and I knew he was going to be in town, so I put a request in with his office that we meet for lunch. His response was simple and direct: "I'm slammed right now. New book underway. Bad time. But ask me again." After feeling peeved for about five seconds, I found I only had more respect for him for so clearly asserting his individual needs.

With so many competing demands for our time and attention, we need to carefully discern who and what we commit to. The question of how to deliver that message—without worrying about what people think, or second-guessing ourselves—is a skill that many of us lack. But it can be learned.

Saying "No" allows you to say "Yes" to other things. By clearly stating what we want and honoring that our needs matter, we can begin to get things done and earn the respect of ourselves and others. And the next time your distant cousin comes to town and you don't feel like meeting up. Just be honest. In the words of Mark Twain: "Tell the truth, it's easier to remember."

# Typecasting

W HEN HE WAS a 9-year-old schoolboy, Neil deGrasse Tyson first visited the Hayden Planetarium in New York. Sure, he had glimpsed at the night sky before, but that was from the rooftop of an apartment building in the Bronx. Never before had he seen the Milky Way like this. Lit up like a Christmas tree inside the planetarium's darkened theater, the night sky had a profound and galvanizing effect on him. He was literally "star struck" by that first encounter with space, and it would change the direction of his life. By the time he was 11, he was telling anyone who would listen that he was going to be an astrophysicist. Pretty precocious, even by 11-year-old standards!

Today, he is the Director of the Hayden Planetarium in New York and one of the country's best-loved and most passionate scientific communicators. I'm struck by two thoughts. 1) How wonderful (and rare) that a boy so young should be so confident of his direction in life, and 2) How easy it would have been for others to discourage him from this foolish childhood notion, and how tragic if that had happened.

In order to achieve his ambition, however, he would need to overcome all manner of societal stereotypes, including the low expectations of teachers who might easily have steered a young black boy from the Bronx towards athletics, and not astrophysics.

Whether we like it or not, we are all being typecast. We get typecast on the basis of our age, gender, race, where we live, or simply by how we look. It's a form of mental shorthand that likes to categorize people quickly and easily. As soon as we put people in a box—no further thought is required. With these easy-to-read labels—Hipster, Party Girl, Retiree, Flake—we make snap judgments about people that precludes any getting to know them. While labels can be useful when buying a tin of soup, they are less so when applied to human beings. When all you see is the "label"—you may miss out on the totality of that person, and the multitudes contained therein.

Lately in my coaching sessions, I've found myself saying "you've been typecast" to clients who may feel frustrated at being misunderstood, forced into a role or treated unfairly. I've seen it come up during mediations, where two co-workers are at loggerheads and wrongly assume they know all there is to know about what the other is thinking. We have a tendency to make assumptions about everything. When this happens, I usually have them drop the script they are holding, and ask open-ended questions of each other. Questions like: "What is really happening for you? How are you feeling? What do you need?" It is surprising how often false assumptions are behind real misunderstandings, and how quickly fear and distrust melt away when two people get to know each other properly for the very first time.

I think we rely on typecasting because we are often in a rush and we have lost some of the art of being curious. It's an easy trap to fall into, especially with those we are closest to. We say things like: "I know what he's thinking; my wife would never go for that;

my boss doesn't like to collaborate; he or she is not the type; my colleagues already know I care about them..." Really? How do you *know*? I, too, sometimes find it difficult to remain fully present and attentive. It takes a strong will not to jump in when someone else is talking. But any time we pigeonhole someone, or finish a sentence for them, or presume to know what their answer will be, we have not only stopped listening. We are typecasting.

## CHANGE THE WAY YOU LOOK AT THINGS AND THE LOOK OF THINGS CHANGE

Sometimes it's a physical distance that allows us to see something old in a new light. Like the first photograph of earth taken from outer space. The famous "Earthrise" photograph—taken aboard Apollo 8 as it orbited the moon in 1968—was the first time anybody had actually seen what our own planet looked like. Prior to this, it only existed as a diagram on schoolroom walls. But with that one color photograph, suddenly we were afforded a new "cosmic" perspective, and it changed the way we think about ourselves and the planet. Says Neil deGrasse Tyson: "We went looking for the moon, but discovered the earth instead."

In the personal realm, sometimes it's a tiny shift in perspective that allows us to see someone familiar in a new and interesting way. It may be watching your spouse or partner interact with someone across a crowded room, and noticing something you hadn't seen before. It may be watching your boss skillfully handle a meeting, and admiring this ability you hadn't seen in the past. Or it may be the "stranger at the dinner table" phenomenon—where suddenly you are amazed to learn more about your parent in 30 minutes than you have in the entire previous 30 years. It's not that anyone necessarily changed in that scenario, it's only the perspective that changed.

When we can resist the urge to typecast, both ourselves and others, we may be surprised by what we see. In the words of Proust: "The real voyage of discovery consists not in seeking out new landscapes, but in having new eyes."

# CHAPTER SIX

# Responsibility

*"Life has no auto-settings. No batteries.*
*You gots to wind it up!"*

—

**Jeb Dickerson**

# A Guide for Grown-ups

A LITTLE OVER FIFTY years ago, a young American president stood in front of the United States Congress to give his inaugural address, exhorting the crowd to "ask not what your country can do for you; ask what you can do for your country." That famous quote—attributed variously to Kahlil Gibran, Cicero, General Omar Bradley, or Milton Friedman, depending on whom you ask— is now part of our shared history. It was a rallying call that launched a new era of responsible citizenship, one in which our participation was required if we wanted a different experience of the world we lived in. These were not "liberal" or "conservative" values, but a belief in the simple idea that as adults, we each have an obligation to pull our own oar.

Being an adult at work means that we bring conscious choice and awareness to our responsibilities. And I believe the future of work demands that we all need to grow up a bit. During my years as a recruiter, and now as an executive coach, I have seen behavior that wouldn't be tolerated in the playground, somehow pass for "normal" in the boardroom. I've seen passive aggressive behavior, as well as "active" aggressive behavior: temper tantrums, tossed tables and chairs (as well as the odd tossed Caesar salad). "Oh, but she's under a lot of stress!" "He's juggling a lot of things at home!" Well, guess what? We're all under a lot of stress. But if you want people to stop treating you like a child, you have to stop acting like one.

I recently conducted a workshop with my friend and fellow coach, Jerry Colonna, where we spoke to a number of executive leaders on this very subject. A lot of these young companies are in an early development phase, and there are tensions and growing pains associated with that. But so many people, in avoidance of individual responsibility, throw up their hands and say, "Well, this problem was caused by somebody else, not me, therefore it's up to him to solve it." No great company, or country, was ever built on this faulty premise. Hence, we have the "new" rules for Grown Ups.

## NO WHINING

Just as Tom Hanks famously declared, "There's no crying in baseball!" There is to be no whining at work. Are there people who enjoy certain advantages over you? Of course there are. Some people are born on third base and think they hit a triple. "But it's not fair," you wail. Well, life's not fair either. Complainers are always making some kind of excuse for why things aren't working out the way they should. Sometimes they will have elaborate and highly "logical" reasons for this. But complainers are rarely successful. You have to be a doer instead. Take all of the latent energy that you put into moaning and divert that into positive forward momentum. Audit your output for one day, and see where you're putting your mental energy. If you're complaining more than you are doing, then it's time for a tune-up.

# CLEAN UP THE MESS
# (EVEN IF YOU DIDN'T MAKE IT)

How many times have you heard someone say, "Don't look at me, that's not my job!" We cannot solve a problem by hoping that someone else is going to figure it out for us. Yet this simple, irascible fact is seemingly beyond the comprehension of much of the human race. If there is something that you have the capacity to fix, and fixing it will improve working conditions for you and others around you, then it is your responsibility to do something about it. Don't wait for them to do it, do it for yourself! Gandhi said we must "be the change we wish to see in the world." If you see an opportunity where you can positively impact your situation (without infringing on others' freedom), then do it. And don't look for accolades. Instead notice how you tend to like yourself more when you choose to act in an adult way.

# NO BLAMING OTHERS *give your power away*

The moment you apportion blame away from yourself and onto someone else, you give away your power. You'll often hear it in the rationalizing phrase: "But I can't do X because of Y." People find it amazing when I point out to them that, by and large, the situation in which they find themselves is often the result of an earlier decision they've made. We are the authors of our lives, and until we realize this, we will always be tempted to blame someone else for what is or isn't working about it. When things don't go your way, instead of protesting and complaining "Why me?" instead ask yourself, "Now what?" This is a giant step into adulthood because it shifts focus onto how we can move on with our life, instead of dwelling on how immobilized we are as victims.

Being an adult isn't easy, especially in the world of work where things may not always go as we would like. But by taking personal responsibility for our choices, we grow and act in ways that we can be proud of. The extent to which we avoid taking responsibility for those choices is the extent to which our lives and relationships will remain dysfunctional.

Your life is not what the stars, your boss, genetics, or the economy decide it will be. It is what you decide it will be.

# Company of One

"**I**'VE ALWAYS BELIEVED that if done properly, armed robbery doesn't have to be a totally unpleasant experience." So says the charming hustler played by Brad Pitt in "Thelma and Louise," a movie that set female hearts a flutter and finally made him a star. I've always felt the same way about "performance reviews" that crop up about once a year in most organizations, to the dread and apprehension of employees. There is no single discussion that causes more anxiety, or that holds so much potential for anger and resentment. But it doesn't have to be that way. For what is a review but a renegotiation of terms? And both sides, if they play their cards right, can benefit enormously from the opportunity this presents.

On the manager's side, a little preparation goes a long way. Some managers like to meet casually, or "on the fly." I knew of one boss who would offer feedback to employees while they rode the elevator up to the 22nd floor, before casually stepping out the door with a clipped "good luck." I've known others who will simply cut and paste last year's review, switch out a few words here and there before hitting "send." The worst part about this approach is that it sends the wrong message by saying, "I'm really busy and important, and I don't have time to think about you and your job." But feedback, if it's to be of any use, needs to be honest, thoughtful, specific and if possible, more positive than negative. Most of us can handle criticism, however painful, if we recognize the truth in it.

A great truism of all critical feedback is that you're probably not as good as you'd hoped, and never really as bad as you think. The truth—for most of us—lies somewhere in between. The "review" is a great opportunity for the employee to elevate her stock, by stating openly her accomplishments. Again, good preparation is key. Focus clearly on your strengths and what you have achieved, and if possible frame it into a compelling narrative that puts you at the center. Whether you're up for advancement or not, this is still a useful exercise. Bragging is allowed here. Unfortunately, most of us tend to remember far better our failures than our successes, so this is helpful to balance our skewed perception of ourselves.

The workplace has changed enormously in recent years. Gone are the days when some benevolent company would direct and manage your career for you, while you dozed off at the wheel. Now more than ever, it is incumbent upon every employee to proactively manage his own career. We have become in essence, a nation of free agents. A company of one. And all successful "companies" must identify and set their priorities in such a way that our goals can be achieved. In the humdrum of work, it's often easy to find yourself adrift, floating aimlessly downstream without clear intent or destination. The days blur into each other, until you have no idea where you are going, or what it was you hoped to achieve. But ask yourself this question: if you're not steering the ship, then who is?

There's a saying that goes "nobody ever stumbled up a mountain." And nobody "accidentally" became famous either, regardless of what he or she may tell you. Even for Brad Pitt, I'm sure it took years of acting classes, silly bit parts and horrible auditions in order to get there. And for you to get where you want to go, you must first identify a destination and then have a clear plan. What does this mean for the modern professional? Well, it means setting out broad career objectives for yourself every year or six months, being alert to opportunities as they arise, and constantly sharpening your skills to meet the moment. I've often heard people confidently say they have "20 years' experience," when what they really have is one year's experience repeated 20 times over.

A performance review is an excellent opportunity for you to look at yourself, and update, if necessary, your individual company's charter. What did I produce this past year? What did I learn? Where am I getting in my own way? Where could I use some help? Is there coaching available in my company? Are there any personal development classes that would make certain parts of my job easier? Should I be speaking with other industry peers in my field so that I remain current? Is there anybody I can identify who might be willing to mentor me while I navigate this tricky next phase of my career?

If you find you are not growing in the way you would like, or you believe your professional goals are not being met, then maybe it's time to look elsewhere. Companies that do right by their employees will generally find their employees trying to do right by the company. But if a company does not look out for its employees, then you can bet that smart employees will likely do what's best for themselves and their families. Don't stick with a company that lacks the opportunities to empower your career progress. If you have a good set of core skills, and know where you want to go, there are many ventures that will want to help you get there.

Bottom line is this: you get what you settle for. Don't settle for less.

# The Denver Test

"**S**o, TELL ME about yourself?"

It's both the easiest and most difficult question in the world to answer. Having worked as an executive recruiter for more than 10 years, I've heard thousands of answers to this question. And often what I was looking for was not actual details, but the manner in which those details were delivered. Is it enthusiastic, inspiring, thoughtful? In an interview, the medium is the message, revealing all kinds of information. Does this person have a healthy self-esteem, a sense of humor? Does he speak confidently, articulately? Is he able to think on his feet and engage in a way that is concise, interesting, and honest? Or did he just put the room to sleep?

One of the recruiters I used to work with had his own formula, jokingly referred to as the Denver Test: "Is this someone I wouldn't mind being stuck with on a four-hour flight to Denver, or do I need to pack a parachute?" Whether you're currently looking for a job or not, it's important to keep those interview skills sharp as you look for the next opportunity.

# THINK CONNECTORS

More than 80% of all jobs are filled by personal referral. That's a fact. What it means is that your cousin's friend, your alumni base, your community 5K race roster, your extended family network, your book club—all are important tools for getting and staying connected to the world of work. A "warm referral" is the greatest gift you can give to someone, because you're putting your own reputation on the line. But if it works out, both parties stand to benefit from the introduction. Give freely and often, and don't worry about getting it back.

# TARGETED AND SPECIFIC

One of the biggest complaints I hear from job hunters is that they get zero response from jobs posted online. This is accurate. Because about 10,000 other people saw the same job listing and also applied. Computer programs root out those with less than a 98% match to the listed job requirements using keywords. It's not ideal, but it's a way for companies to cast a very wide net then filter what they catch extremely quickly. You need to be very targeted in your approach, and fortunately, there has never been an easier time to do this. If you can find somebody on LinkedIn at the company you're interested in working for, ask for an informational meeting to "pick their brain" on corporate culture, their own career, or whatever it is. If that goes well, who knows? It may lead to an actual introduction to a hiring manager. But don't leave it up to chance, or worse, computer programs.

## WHAT'S YOUR STORY?

What is the story you are telling about yourself? I've written in the past about "story fondling" and how it can hurt us. The dating metaphor is apt here. You don't want to reveal your ugly divorce story on the first date. Nobody wants to hear how your last boss was a narcissist who stole your retirement when he went off his meds in Cancun and embezzled company funds. Or how your great idea was stolen, and now you're too old to do anything about it because "the goalposts have shifted." People don't want drama, they want creative solutions to their immediate problems. So leave old baggage behind, and reframe your résumé as an "adventure story" that someone might be interested in hearing. And keep it concise: know when to stop talking. Whatever the content, the tone of your story must be positive, hopeful, and forward-focused.

## DON'T FORGET THE BASICS

Good basic manners still count for a lot. That means confirming your appointment, showing up ahead of time, and being overdressed rather than underdressed. If you are meeting with a Fortune 500 company, you'd better be well-versed in any recent press, positive or negative. Understanding the "prevailing winds" shows you are interested and have done your homework. It may sound obvious, but a well-written, snail-mailed thank-you note is as rare as it is effective. I have always remembered those candidates who wrote to express gratitude after they had landed in a position. It's about respect for people's time, and treating everyone you meet with dignity, whether they can help you or not. As the saying goes, "Be nice to the people you meet on the way up, because you might meet them again on the way down."

## IT'S ONLY A CONVERSATION

Think of every meeting you have as a "conversation," not an interrogation. The goal is to keep the conversation going and make it pleasant and memorable for everyone. Body language is about 80% of how you are perceived, so be cognizant of what your eyes, hands and nails are doing. If you're in career transition, can you see this period of limbo as an opportunity to share, learn, and grow? Devote only a portion of your day to the job search, and the rest to developing interests that enhance your value as a whole person. Travel, reading, volunteering—all make you more interesting and give you something to talk about. Sometimes a small part-time hustle can turn into a full-time job. (If you haven't already, I highly recommend you check out the documentary film *Lemonade*.)

People don't really care about what you "do," they care about who you are and what you're passionate about. Like the old maxim says, "People don't hire résumés, people hire people." The good news is that regardless of where you find yourself, we all have the ability to be a good travel companion on that four-hour flight to Denver.

# Adaptation

WHILE I AM not usually drawn to military memoirs, I found I could not put down General Stanley McChrystal's *Team of Teams: New Rules of Engagement For a Complex World.* The book is an easy read, even for military know-nothings like myself. He does a masterful job of telling his own story, while extrapolating from it some great lessons in leadership and organizational change. He tells how when he took over in Iraq, he found the traditional "centralized management style" of the U.S. Army no longer worked against the more fluid and agile enemy of Al Qaeda. The challenge was obvious, and stark: adapt quickly or die.

In *Team of Teams*, he challenges leaders to create organizations that are more nimble, transparent, horizontal rather than hierarchical, and that empower their people to execute based on the concept of a "shared consciousness." In other words, help people to understand the common goal, and then empower them to do their jobs to the best of their ability. In the tech startup world where I often circulate, "agile" is a buzzword I often hear bandied about. It describes a similar adaptive quality that allows companies to detect changes on the wind, and make corrective adjustments almost in real time.

One of the great business blunders of recent times is the way Kodak failed to understand the digital revolution that was sweeping the photographic industry that they helped to pioneer. Kodak's inability (or unwillingness) to change their business model from the highly profitable film model to pixels, would ultimately cause them to go bankrupt. With the benefit of hindsight, it seems almost laughable that such an innovative company could be so blind to changes on the wind, but I think it perfectly illustrates the enormous challenge of organizational change. Human beings possess an almost uncanny ability to *resist* change at all costs. But change we must, if we are to survive. What are some of the ways we can do this?

**1. Do Not Fear Change, Fear Not Changing**

For any change to occur, the people at the top have to at least be open to change. Ironically, the more success you achieve—either as an individual or a company—the harder it can be to accept change. We become invested in doing things one way "because it worked for us in the past." This is the kind of thinking that got Kodak into trouble. Unlike their founder, George Eastman, who was a great innovator, Kodak's management team in the 90's was unwilling to consider digital as a replacement for film. We invented this technology, they thought, and by golly people like it! But tastes change over time, as well as the technology. By resisting the natural shift that was happening all around them, they failed to respond effectively. By the time they decided to jump on board with the digital revolution, the ship had already sailed.

**2. When the Landscape Changes, Get a New Roadmap**

The best companies—the ones that survive over the long haul—are constantly evolving in new and interesting ways. Being able to adapt the business plan to changing conditions on the ground is key. Problems arise when someone refuses to give up the map, even when it's obvious the map is wholly outdated, or worse—was never accurate to begin with. It is the courageous leader who will stand up and say, "You know what, this isn't working for us anymore. I think we need to change direction." Often, change is very difficult for organizations because there are egos involved. There may be money already spent, and they fear the deep negative costs of an about-face: *how much* is this going to cost me? But often the cost of not changing, when it is clearly indicated, will be higher.

### 3. Increase Your Exposure

Our muscles become stiff if we don't exercise them now and again. So too with our organizations: a lack of "stretch" leads to rigidity over time, and rigid structures can often suffer from tunnel vision. One way to increase your flexibility is to deliberately put yourself into a position where you must use your adaptive muscles. Maybe instead of always staying at the Marriott, which you know and like, you could try Airbnb? Instead of taking the same vacation, which you know and like, you might try a different location? The only way to grow our adaptive muscles is to flex them now and again, and that means occasionally we must increase our exposure to new people, new ideas, new ways of looking at the world. By gradually increasing our exposure to ambiguity, our minds are forced to remain open, curious, agile.

### 4. Challenge All Assumptions

Over the course of many years as a recruiter, and then as a coach, I've had the opportunity to engage with a lot of different companies and leaders. More than any other trait, I find it is the quality of intellectual curiosity that separates the good from the great. To be curious is to challenge deeply held assumptions, even habits they've engaged in for years, and ask "Is this the best way forward?" Of course, this implies a certain level of humility. It says, "The world is complex and rapidly changing, and what worked for us in the past, may not work in the future."

Bottom line: Darwin was right. All of us must constantly adapt, or face possible extinction.

# Batteries Not Included

**O**NE OF MY clients came to see me under orders from his employer. His last position in sales hadn't worked out too well, and a recent string of development meetings had failed to produce any tangible results. His boss was concerned, and asked if I would I connect with him to see if he was somehow sending out the "wrong signals." On the surface at least, this young man was well-qualified and well-dressed. When I asked how things were going, he slouched back on the couch in my office and said, "I'm bored." And how is your boss to work for, I inquired. "My boss? She's an ass." What about the company, what is the work environment like? "It sucks." Every question was met with a similar monosyllabic response: lame, awful, nightmare, and so on.

Back when I worked in recruitment, the term we euphemistically used to describe a candidate like this was "low-energy." A person's "vibe," while hard to define, is instantly recognizable the moment it walks in the door. We may not be able to see it, but we sure can feel it. Negative energy has the effect of instantly making you feel tired because it sucks all of the life force out of a room. Positive energy, by contrast, enhances and brightens the room. It adds something to the equation instead of subtracting.

Positive energy

The act of extending oneself requires expending some energy, moving against our own natural inclination to conserve energy. As we do this, little things begin to change. Did you ever notice how one positive interaction with another person can alter the tenor of your day? It happens. Someone smiles at you for no obvious reason, or pays you an unexpected compliment, and suddenly the world looks a bit different. Well here's a little secret: your entire life is like this. What you sow, you will reap. The energy you put out into the world—in the shape of your thoughts, your words, your action—will largely determine your experience of life and the opportunities you attract into it.

## GIVE IT AWAY

The way to get more energy is to expend more energy. It seems counter-intuitive but it's not. When I don't feel like exercising (which is often), the biggest challenge for me is simply getting my running shoes on and heading out the door. Once I'm out there, my well of energy fills. The same holds true for anything that you want to attract more of. Want more love and affection in you life? You need to give more love and affection to people. Want better leadership in your job? Then act like a better leader. Want more respect from your peers? Then give more respect to those around you. Want to feel inspired? Be someone who inspires others. Whatever it is that you feel you are lacking, give it away, freely and often. You will get it back in buckets.

## PUT YOUR WHOLE HEART INTO IT

The way to get buy-in and commitment from others is to wholly commit yourself. I remember watching an interview with actor

Daniel Day-Lewis. The interviewer was asking him, with some faint derision, about his torturous method of preparation for playing any role. His answer was simple and brilliant: "How can I expect anyone to believe me in a role if I don't first believe it myself?" We need to commit fully to the part we're playing and believe that the things we say are important to us. But how often do we really do this? How often do we follow through with our whole hearts and minds? Are we really trying or are we holding back just a little bit? While we may not succeed, no failure is ever a total failure if we have put forth an honest effort with all our heart. Then we can sleep well at night knowing we did our best.

## NURTURE YOUR RELATIONSHIPS

I don't know what the exact nature of your business is, but I can tell you with absolute certainty what the key to it is: people. It's about building solid relationships, nurturing them, and maintaining them as best you can. And how do we do this? By bringing positive intention to all our interactions so that people do not feel depleted after having met us. By returning phone calls on time; by acting nobly and professionally; by not badmouthing others behind their backs. By being present and actively listening to our colleagues. By treating others the same way we want to be treated, even when things don't work out. Think of it as a garden. Where we put our attention, things will grow. Where we don't, things wither and die away.

Every day, we are faced with a simple choice about how we are going to be in the world. And it usually boils down to this: am I the one bringing positive energy to the table, or am I taking it away? Am I a part of the problem, or the solution?

We have been given the greatest gift of all, but it does not come with batteries included. YOU have to supply those. In the words of Jeb Dickerson: "Life has no auto-settings. No batteries. You gots to wind it up!"

I have to be, t
do it
to Have it)

# Win-Win:
# How to Succeed at Almost Anything
## (Hint: It Starts with Helping Others Succeed)

OVER THE YEARS, I've written about interview techniques and negotiation tactics, all useful for finding our way into a job. Harder than actually getting hired though, is staying hired once someone says "yes." Then the real work begins, navigating uncharted waters in sometimes hostile territory where we don't always know the rules.

While it may be a gross oversimplification, I often say that there are two main drivers for people at work: fear and desire. Most of what we do is determined by one or the other. We fear criticism, disapproval, being taken advantage of, being taken for granted. We desire recognition, status, security, and understanding. Both are powerful motivators in the short term, but only one will help you succeed over the long haul. (Hint: it's not fear).

This is why it is vitally important to keep our minds firmly fixed on the things we actually want, rather than what we don't want. Most happy, effective people recognize the inherent power of their own thoughts, and have learned ways to harness this power to their advantage. You want to be continually moving in the direction you want to go (desire), while tuning out or minimizing the fear. If you're looking for ways to succeed at work, here are some simple strategies to keep in mind.

## IT'S NOT ALL ABOUT YOU

The single greatest thing you can do to succeed in any job is to help those around you succeed at theirs. I'm not talking about brown-nosing or buying people elaborate holiday gifts. I'm talking about a deep commitment to the work you have taken on, and a conscientious desire to make life easier for those around you. This means anticipating needs before they arise, going the extra mile, protecting other people's interests (and secrets), and doing your absolute best because you want your team or organization to succeed as a whole. If you do that, your value will skyrocket, and your boss will look good for simply having hired you. When they win, you win.

## MANAGE YOURSELF FIRST

It's almost impossible to manage others well unless you first learn how to effectively manage yourself. Sounds obvious, but it's harder to put into practice. Managing yourself means bringing a keen sense of awareness to how you show up for work. Are you getting enough rest? Are you looking after your health? Are you in touch with your emotions? Are you open to receiving feedback, or are you easily triggered? Often I meet with clients who assume that everyone around them is causing problems, when in fact the complete opposite is true. Begin with YOURSELF, and go from there. A commitment to doing some form of "inner work" (in the form of coaching or therapy) is usually the first step to doing good outer work.

## TWO SOLUTIONS FOR EVERY PROBLEM

Problems are a part of every work environment. Finding solutions to those problems (or at least minimizing them) should be your goal. You want to be the kind of person who generally brings more solutions to the table than problems, by a margin of at least two-to-one. We all know workers who love to point out everything that's going wrong without a single idea for how to put it right. The company is going down the tubes, things are getting worse, the sky is always falling. Don't become that person, and don't associate with people who are willing you (and the company) to fail. As the saying goes, "If you're not a part of the solution, you are a part of the problem."

## COMMITMENT TO THE PROCESS

While goals are certainly useful, your commitment to the overall process of achieving them is the greater predictor of a successful outcome. Here, the "three P's" come into play: practice, patience, and persistence. You must be willing to persevere for a long time without much evidence of progress. Can you do that? What you're aiming for is not an overnight miracle, but a slow, long-term improvement in the overall quality of your life. Becoming the kind of person (or coworker) you want to be—someone who believes in themselves and believes in others—is more about daily commitment to good process and less about the end product.

# BELIEVE THAT YOU CAN SUCCEED

The ability to do anything must be supported by the belief that we *can* do it. In the words of Henry Ford: "Whether you think you can or think you can't, you're usually right." Yet you'd be amazed by the number of people I see standing in their own way, talking themselves out of raises, promotions, funding, and more. You have to remain open and positive, surround yourself with people who also believe that you can succeed. Most of us are like chameleons: we easily adopt the attitudes, behaviors, and opinions of those we associate with most closely. This is why it's crucial to identify, model, and associate with people who bring out the very best in us.

And finally, I would just say, "Don't take yourself too seriously." The workplace doesn't have to be 100% humorless all the time. Even just a smile reminds everyone that we're not exclusively working beings, we are first and foremost *human* beings. And by helping others succeed at their jobs, we become better at our own jobs. Fear or desire, the choice is always ours.

"Live your life," Rumi reminded us, "as if everything is rigged in your favor."

128

# CHAPTER SEVEN

# Inspiration

*"If you have built castles in the air,*
*your work need not be lost; that is where they should be.*
*Now put the foundations under them."*

—

Henry David Thoreau

# Castles in the Air

$\mathbf{A}$s a child, Foster Huntington dreamed of living in a treehouse. Now, at the ripe old age of 27, he divides his time between two adjoining treehouses—one to live in, the other to work in—both perched precariously on a grassy hilltop overlooking the vast wilderness of the Columbia River Gorge in Washington state. What started out as a young man's pipe dream soon became a plan, which then became a reality, thanks to the help of some willing friends and a bit of clever engineering. An avid outdoorsman and photographer, he is now a social media entrepreneur who runs his empire from up in the canopy, the whimsical treehouses serving as both an inspiring backdrop for his work and a clever advertisement for himself and his brand.

Like all passion projects, this one was not realized overnight. Four years ago, Huntington was living the life of a worker bee in the fashion industry in New York. But something about the urban life and glitzy career did not seem to fit. It began to chafe, like an ill-fitting suit. So after quitting his job at Ralph Lauren, he bought a used VW van and hit the road. He drove around the country taking photographs of "vanlife," living on a steady diet of bean burritos. The photographs turned into a blog, which then turned into a book. The advance from the book gave him the money to turn the dream of building his big-boy treehouse into a reality.

## EXECUTION TRUMPS IDEA

Most people have their own version of a "treehouse" waiting to be built. It could be a book long talked about but never written, a company never started, a widget never invented, an early retirement—some foolish notion that for whatever reason, takes up real estate in our heads and won't let go. Back in 2012, I gave a TEDx talk in the Netherlands where the theme of the conference was "Full Creative Potential." One of the things I spoke about was the necessity of having a good idea, but more importantly, having the ability to properly execute on that idea. Ideas alone are worthless. Without the ability to execute, they remain as castles in the air.

Back when I started my own coaching practice, it took a lot of time and energy to get going. And I had a full-time job at the same time. So I started very small, giving myself the goal of one paying client by the end of the year. One client turned into two, and on it went from there. But it was really difficult in the beginning, and lonely too. Starting a business, I soon realized, is way harder than it looks. Nobody gives you anything, you have to go out there and get it. Thomas Edison once said: "A lot of people miss opportunity because it's dressed in overalls and looks like hard work." And becoming an entrepreneur, starting a business or building a treehouse—is really hard work. This is the execution part where most people fall down.

## YOU WILL NEVER BE READY

"But I'm not ready, I need to do more research, I need to talk to more people," I hear you say. That may be true. But if you have an idea or a project you wish to explore, my advice is simply to begin it. That's it. Begin *before you're ready*. Allowing yourself the possibility of failure is key to getting going. One of the things I liked about Foster Huntington's story was how loosely he approached his tree-house ambition. He didn't overanalyze it, or do market research on treehouses, or write up a business plan. One day, he simply called up one of his buddies and said, "dude, I think I want to build a treehouse." The reason he was able to find people willing to help him was because it was a fun idea. Who doesn't want to build a treehouse? I'm sure that there were challenges and setbacks along the way, but once that initial spark of a creative idea was ignited, there was no going back.

If you have an idea for a project, spec out the minimal features you will need, find some friends willing to help you, or find a single customer willing to pay and just get started. Even if you're not 100% ready. It doesn't have to be perfect. In fact, it might be better if it fails on the first go round. Thomas J. Watson, the founder of IBM put it this way: "Do you want to succeed? Then double your rate of failure. Success lies on the far side of failure."

One of the most damaging myths our culture propagates is this idea of overnight success. But dig a little deeper into any "overnight" success story, and what you will usually find is some obstinate individual who was willing to devote a decade's worth of hard work and perseverance in pursuit of their ambition. It's about making a start, learning from past mistakes, incremental improvements over a period of time. These small daily wins add up like compound interest in a bank.

How and where will you build your treehouse? What does it look like? How will you feel once it's there? In the words of Thoreau: "If you have built castles in the air, that is where they should be. Now put foundations under them."

# The Art of Make Believe

Not long ago, I found myself listening with fascination to a radio piece on NPR about a family growing up in Chicago during the 1980's. The father, Jim Steinfel, had been in the Navy as a young man. Now married with 12 children (yes, that's right, *twelve* children), he invented an elaborate game in order to amuse, distract and occupy his children during the long summer months when they were out of school. All of the kids were enlisted to work on board a ship that he built for them. But this was no ordinary ship. Measuring 24 feet in length and painted battleship gray, the USS Elizabeth was made entirely out of plywood. And even though it had a rudder and an engine room, this ship never sailed. In fact, it never left their suburban back yard.

Think of what a stroke of parenting genius this is if you have a dozen kids all looking at you for something to do. On board the ship, all kids had to wear a uniform—white sailor hats, black neckerchiefs. As in the real Navy, there were rules and responsibilities too. The ship had a strict chain of command and even a mission statement: "To defend Park Ridge's strategic Continental Divide against surprise naval attack." And each kid had an important role to play. There was a captain of course, a gunner's mate, a cook, a radio operator, a boson and a medic. Together, they swabbed the decks, hoisted flags, prepared food in the chow line while waiting for their "deployment" orders to come through. In order to keep their skills sharp, they ran practice drills: a surprise attack, man overboard, storm coming, etc.

As I listened to this beautiful story, I was struck by a couple of things. First and foremost, is the love and affection this father must have had for his children in order to spend the necessary time on this elaborate fiction. The second thing that struck me was the sheer level of detail that went into creating this rich fantasy world—no detail too small to be overlooked. A blender mounted to a wall provided the necessary "engine noise." The life vests and flags were all real, bought from an army-navy store. A working intercom connected the various compartments. An actual captain's log from the U.S. Navy recorded all of the ship's activities.

So what was this father up to? Well, I'm guessing that the overwhelming demand of parenting 12 children required an enormous act of ingenuity in order to safely occupy them. But more than that, I think he wanted to teach his kids how to be disciplined, competent and industrious citizens. He wanted them to be imaginative, and to serve something bigger than just themselves. He wanted them to know the joy of camaraderie, the value of teamwork, the importance of getting the smaller details right. In effect, he wanted them to know that each job on board the ship, no matter how mundane or seemingly unimportant, had intrinsic value.

And I think we want the exact same thing as adults. We want to know that our work is valued and that our role is important. We want to believe that there is meaning in mundane chores performed over and over again. We want to know that we serve some larger purpose. But it becomes much harder once we reach adulthood and enter into the "real" world. A project that we worked on for many years eventually comes to naught, and worse, nobody even notices or cares. A solution that you came up with is met with casual indifference, until somebody else takes credit for it. These are everyday occurrences as an adult, and can be deeply demoralizing.

Jim Steinfel died in 2011. It was interesting to hear his children, now fully grown, talking about how their experiences on board the USS Elizabeth had shaped them as adults. Turns out their father wasn't just reliving his glory days in the navy, he was carefully preparing them for theirs. It was here that they learned about work ethic and discipline and teamwork.

For most of them, the ship began to lose some of its magic by the time they reached puberty. One by one, they would each request a "formal discharge" and go off to pursue other interests. But while they may have left the ship behind, the ship did not leave them. Not surprisingly, four of the children went on to join the Marine Corps. One of them even remarking how life on an actual ship was "not too different" from life onboard the USS Elizabeth!

Whether telling a story, starting a business or imagining a naval vessel into existence—it's the level of *detail* that will ultimately determine its success or failure. Our job is not to worry about whether the ship can sail, but to focus on doing our part, and getting the details right. That's why we need make believe. That's why we need magic. It teaches us how to live.

# P.S. Rocky Didn't Win

LINDSAY DORAN IS a highly successful Hollywood movie producer. With a string of hits to her name that includes *Sense and Sensibility, The Firm, Sabrina, Stranger than Fiction* and *Nanny McPhee*, even some of her "misses" could be considered hits. Last year, I was fortunate enough to hear her speak at the Austin Film Festival on a panel entitled "The Soul of Story." (I was visiting here as the "plus one" with my husband.) She spoke passionately for 90 minutes without so much as a sip of water or a glance at her notes. You could hear a pin drop in the room.

Doran became interested some years ago in the "Positive Psychology" movement pioneered by Martin Seligman. In his book *Flourish*, Dr. Seligman identifies five particular qualities that he says make life worth living: Positive emotions, engagement, positive accomplishments, positive relationships and meaning. To her great surprise, Doran found these to be the exact same things that she considers to be essential ingredients of a good movie. Her research led her to the American Film Institute's list of the 100 most inspirational movies where she broke down the emotional components of our favorite movies in order to test her hypothesis. And what she found surprised her.

Yes, we care when watching a character attempt to learn something new (*The Karate Kid*), achieve an impossible goal (*The King's
Speech*) or heal a broken relationship (*Terms of Endearment*). We also
like movies where people find meaning for their lives (*Erin Brokov-
ich*), or do something really dangerous and heroic (*Die Hard*). But
more than that, what we really care about is the *sharing* of that accomplishment with the people they love, after the fact. Yes, it's great
that King George VI finally gives a speech without stammering, but
what we really want to know is that he and his speech therapist
Lionel remained friends after the fact. It's cool that John McClane
defeats the bad guys, but what we really want to see is the moment
where he is finally reunited with his wife.

Or consider the example of *Rocky* (the original one). A much
beloved classic about a washed-up boxer who goes 15 rounds with
the heavyweight champion of the world. It's number 4 on the AFI's
list of most inspirational movies of all time. It also took home three
Oscars that year, including one for best picture. But what most people forget is that Rocky didn't actually win his fight with Apollo
Creed. He lost! The movie ends in his defeat, also the most exalted
moment of his life, as he proudly declares his love for Adrian. In the
end, the result didn't matter. It is only the relationship that matters:
between Rocky and himself, between Rocky and Adrian.

What these movies reinforce, and what smart people already
know, is that positive relationships trump positive accomplishments
every single time. Simply put: it's not about the prize, it's about the
people. According to Doran, it's not even necessary for uplifting
movies to have happy endings. Some of the most inspirational movies of all time are about loss on a grand scale. In Ms. Doran's words:
"Obi-Wan dies, Dumbledore dies, Gandalf dies, 1500 passengers go
down with the Titanic and thousands of Pandorans die."

What this suggests is that one of the qualities that audiences most enjoy watching is resilience. The quality of "keeping going," even in the face of crushing disappointment. I checked out the AFI's list for myself, and it's interesting to note how many of the characters we know and love do not ultimately get what they want.

George Bailey in *It's a Wonderful Life* does not get to travel around the world. Atticus Finch in *To Kill a Mockingbird* does not win acquittal for his client. Eliot does not get to keep his extraterrestrial friend in *E.T.* Some of the greatest love stories of all time are about lovers who can never be together: *Casablanca, Roman Holiday, Ghost, Love Story.* These are all stories about "letting go."

I am very privileged in my work as a coach to hear people's stories. And having done this for a while now, it seems we all struggle with similar stuff: how to reinvent ourselves and start anew, how to get along with people who are difficult, how to give our lives meaning. I don't have all the answers (I wish I did), but I strongly suspect it has to do with looking for (and finding) those same qualities in ourselves that we so enjoy watching in others: the keeping going despite the setbacks, pushing past limitations, learning to do new things that are scary, showing up for others when it's not always convenient or easy.

Ultimately, the person with the most power over our lives will always be the one staring back at us in the bathroom mirror every morning. Not Apollo Creed, our boss, our spouse, our parents or anyone else. We are the hero of our own story, if we choose to be.

Maybe it ends in victory, maybe it ends in defeat. In the end, the result doesn't even matter. It is the quality of the relationships that we leave behind that makes champions of us all.

# Just Show Up

THIS PAST WEEK, I heard a song playing in Starbucks that stopped me in my tracks. At first I couldn't quite place it, but then I quickly recognized the voice of James Maddock, a terrifically gifted singer/songwriter that I've known for years here in New York. He even played at my birthday party once. But hearing him on the radio like this for the first time literally gave me goose bumps. "Ah," I thought to myself. "He's finally arrived!"

But like a lot of "overnight success" stories, James is no stranger to heartache. Which may be why his songs are so damn good. Signed to Columbia records at a young age, he was then unceremoniously dumped when his first record didn't sell well. But he never stopped believing in his talent. Writing, gigging, recording demos when he could afford to—he gradually honed his craft to perfection over a period of ten years or more. And the result is a dreamy new album of songs called *Sunrise on Avenue C* which if you're lucky, you may hear in your local coffee shop. You might even catch him in concert, that is, if you can squeeze through the door.

While not new, I believe his story is instructive for many reasons. The problem with most of us is that we simply give up too soon. Or too easily. What James's story exemplifies for me is persistence. It's about showing up for the gig when there are only four people in the pub. It's about performing at the highest level when there appears to be no obvious reward. Why? Because you're a professional. And that's what professionals do: they show up.

Back when I was running a lot of marathons, I discovered that most of the battle in training was simply getting beyond my own mood. A lot of the time, I didn't even feel like running. I'd be about to lace up my shoes, when suddenly I'd think of a hundred reasons why I shouldn't go. Similarly, on race day, I never felt fully prepared. But by virtue of just putting one foot in front of the other—I got myself out there. We're usually told that action follows motivation—when in fact it's often the other way around. Action first, and the motivation or insight typically follows.

In 1987, when my brother Walter was graduating from The Cooper Union and interviewing for jobs, the market for engineers was grim. He tells a story of having an early interview scheduled one Friday morning following a rowdy all-night party with some of his fraternity brothers. When he awoke the day of the interview, he felt like death warmed over. But something told him he needed to show up anyway. If someone was going to give him their time, he felt it important to honor that commitment, regardless of how bad he felt. Luckily he did, and the rest is history. He's been with the same firm for 25 years where he is now a senior partner. That little effort, which he could easily have not made, changed the course of his life.

I recently asked Nicole DeBoom, ironwoman competitor and founder of Skirt Sports if she could describe a time for me when she showed up for something that had impacted her life in a positive way. She admitted that this pretty much happens every day. She is a big believer in connecting with everyone she meets. Sitting in a middle seat on the airplane should always be accompanied

141

by this thought, "today I'm very lucky. I get to meet not one, but TWO, potentially great people." On one such trip, Nicole sat next to the man who would later become her husband. So her advice is to always engage with the people next to you. You never know who might just appear!

One of the things I hear in my career coaching practice when clients are exploring new options is some variation of the theme "But I'm just not ready!" To which I always reply, "neither am I!" One of the great lessons I learned from a public speaking class I took last year was to "trust in the moment." The best communication happens when we let down our guard and allow the experience to unfold in its own way—even when we may not be 100% prepared. If you feel lost, lousy, or clumsy—say so, but don't let it stand in the way of your showing up. We're not here to put on masks; we're here to live, learn, and share a little piece of ourselves.

I've noticed that what typifies people who don't lose heart in spite of challenging setbacks, is that they tend to focus on small, achievable goals that can be reached on a daily basis. And typically, they don't dwell too much on the difficulty of their situation (what I like to call "story fondling"). Instead, they learn to stay forward-focused, and harness their energy for what can be done. Even if you don't feel like doing anything, maybe there is just one thing that you can do that will move you closer to where you need to go. And in doing that one thing, you will muster the inspiration to do the next thing.

I have many days when I am not driven to show up for a task. But over time, I've found that I don't always have to feel like it. Nor is it always necessary to be fully prepared, or perfectly groomed, or feeling on top of the world. Nobody feels that way all of the time. What is essential is that we open the window to allow for the possibility of good things to enter. Each new day, and each new opportunity is a chance to practice this. And practice is what makes perfect. Just ask James Maddock. The long road to Carnegie Hall begins with showing up. Because you know what happens when you don't?

That's right: absolutely nothing.

# Double Down

$I$N A RECENT article by the Wall Street Journal, *The Shawshank Redemption* is cited as one of the most profitable movies of all time. A full twenty years after its release, it is still making heaps of money. With its universal themes of hope, friendship and perseverance, it is also one of the most beloved movies by critics and audiences alike. While its slow-burning success may seem obvious in retrospect, it was anything but preordained when screenwriter Frank Darabont first floated the script around Hollywood.

As the story goes, there was keen interest from several studios, including Castle Rock Entertainment who wanted Rob Reiner to direct the movie. Mr. Darabont was made an offer that would have made him a multi-millionaire, in return for his handing over of the script and the rights to the story. After taking a night to think about it, Mr. Darabont refused the offer, insisting instead that he be allowed to direct his own script for a greatly reduced fee. In the end, he decided that his "passion for the project was not for sale." It turned out to be a very smart decision for him, and Castle Rock.

I work with a lot of startup companies where the attrition rate for ideas is pretty high. About 3 out of every 4 venture-backed businesses will ultimately fail. When I started my own coaching practice back in 2005, it was anything but certain. I gave up a good salary and benefits in order to pursue my ambition of working for myself. And it seems to me that in order to achieve your ultimate dream, be it a business or any creative endeavor, you may need to "double down"—which often means prioritizing long-term goals over short-term gains. In short, you really need to back yourself first. What are some of the ways in which we can do this?

## DECIDE WHAT YOU WANT

Sounds easy, but it's actually a huge risk to name the thing you want, which is why so many people have a hard time doing it. What if you don't get it? Will you look like a failure? Mr. Darabont had a very clear idea of what he wanted to achieve for his film, and that drove all his decision-making. You must decide what you want before you determine how to get it. In my own case, it was autonomy, flexibility and the desire to help people that led me to pursue coaching. But I had to name it first, and that took some time and soul searching. Figure out what you want, and then take a chance and write it down. Write the business plan or book proposal that you've been mulling over. If you don't know where you want to go, it's highly unlikely that you will ever get there.

## INVEST IN YOURSELF

If you're not willing to invest in yourself, then ask yourself, why should anybody else? Investing in yourself can take many forms: developing healthier eating habits and exercise routines; taking the time to learn new skills; apprenticing yourself to a mentor; raising your hand to take on new responsibilities. If you find you're not getting the right kind of support or training you need from your employers, then invest in your own training to help you acquire the skills you need to succeed. I have personally invested thousands of dollars and hundreds of hours on training and personal development courses in order to grow my business and better serve my clients. Each time I do this, I am investing in myself and my future.

## SEE IT DONE

While I'm certainly no mystic, I firmly believe in the power of visualization to change hearts and lives. It begins by creating a very clear picture in your mind of the completed goal, and imagining how that will make you feel. Each time you visualize this goal, you strengthen your resolve and intensify your desire to achieve it. This is why it is vitally important to focus on things you want, rather than what you don't want. (It's also why some people become the very thing they fear.) Think of your mind as computer, you are the programmer who creates the operating system. You want to make sure that the software you are running supports your ultimate ambition, and is not infected by "malware." Henry Ford put it this way: "Whether you think you can, or you think you can't—you're usually right."

## PERSISTENCE REAPS RESULTS

In the difficult decisions I've made through the course of building my business, I often never feel brave. In fact, sometimes I'm scared to death. Persistence is the ability to keep pursuing your goals in spite of fear or adversity. It means you press on even when you feel like quitting. Though your motivation may wax and wane over time, you know that deep down if you keep doing the right actions, you'll eventually get the results you want. Persistence, ultimately, is an act of faith (I believe I can do this), and a gift we give to ourselves (I believe I am worthy of this). And it comes from a vision of the future that is so compelling you would do almost anything to make it a reality. In this way, all great companies are made. And in this way, a man with a six-inch rock hammer can tunnel his way out of prison after twenty years of incarceration.

Remember, when the chips are down, always...always bet on yourself.

① Name it
② Write it down
③ Mentor
④ Invest in training
⑤ ≠ Envision it done / Test past

# CHAPTER EIGHT

# Gratitude

*"Gratitude makes sense of our past, brings peace for today, and creates a vision for tomorrow."*

———

**Melody Beattie**

# A Guide to Recognizing Your Saints

IF YOU WORK with people who are in career transition, as I often do, you end up hearing a lot of interesting stuff about what goes on inside companies. There are many reasons why a person might decide to leave one job to pursue another. Often there are grievances involved. But far and away the commonest reason I hear for people quitting their jobs—is a lack of recognition and acknowledgment for work they have done. Time and again I hear things like: "It would have been nice to have gotten a pat on the back once in a while. You know, it was the kind of place where you rarely heard the word *thanks*. I never knew if my contribution mattered. The only time I ever heard from my boss was if I did something wrong."

As children, we demand to be noticed: "Look at the brilliant sandcastle I built! Watch me ride my bike off the roof of the garage!" As adults, we are (hopefully) focused on different things, but the need to be recognized for our efforts does not diminish over time. People want to know that their contribution counts for something. We long to know that the mountain of hours and years of service devoted to some cause or company does not go unnoticed by someone. But far too often it does. And what happens then? Petty resentments build. Morale wanes. And good performers leave in search of greater fulfillment and appreciation elsewhere.

If you're a manager or leader of any sort, you know who your saints are: those quiet, diligent, unshowy performers who are with you through thick and thin. This is the kind of person you want to have in the raft beside you when the ship is going down. And it's easy to take these people for granted. Maybe we're too busy, or too tired. We get distracted. We have a demanding new client who is sucking the energy from us. But these people are your life preservers, and it behooves you to acknowledge them. If you're going to give recognition, here are some important things to keep in mind.

## BE HONEST

People like to know where they stand, so tell them, as often as you can. Dr. Colleen Hacker, sports psychologist to the U.S. Women's National Soccer Team, is a big believer in giving honest performance-contingent comments to her team directly after each game and training session. She rewards effort as much as outcome and uses a technique she likes to call "the feedback sandwich". Here's how it works:

1. Find something the player did well and then praise it. *positive*
2. Next, tell the athlete what they did incorrectly, and how they can improve on it next time. *negatively*
3. Finish with a positive, encouraging or motivational statement. One piece of negative sandwiched between two positively reinforcing statements. Her impressive results speak for themselves. *positively*

## BE THOUGHTFUL

It's interesting how many of the managers I know will spend literally hours preparing to give criticism to subordinates, but only a matter of minutes preparing to give praise for what was done right. Thoughtful praise should get the exact same consideration as negative criticism. Nobody wants insincere flattery, but a genuine appreciation of the effort put forth can go a long way toward boosting morale and improving overall performance. Find a way of noticing some particular detail that lets people know they are seen. E.G. "When I showed our new client the research you had compiled, they were really impressed. They want a follow-up proposal for a further piece of business. That's a really good outcome for us, so thank you and well done!"

## CELEBRATE SMALL WINS

As any parent will tell you, celebrating the small gains is an important part of building confidence and reinforcing positive behavior. I'm not talking about being cheered just for turning up to work in the morning. But taking the time to celebrate small victories as they occur—a new client is landed, a report goes out on time, a killer presentation—is vitally important. And a series of small victories often becomes a big victory. Ask any winning team—sports or otherwise—and they will tell you that success breeds more success. Once people get a taste for winning, it makes them hungry for more. So take the time to celebrate the small wins, as much as the big ones.

## ATTITUDE OF GRATITUDE

If your business is about people (and what business isn't?), then you need to pay very close attention to who is doing the actual work in your company. Even saints don't like being ignored! You can say it with a smile, a kind word, or the ultimate—a handwritten note. It says: You count. I see your effort. Yes, it matters. Although they may not show it, you never know how much someone may be needing this.

Even if you're not getting it for yourself, the unselfish act of giving praise freely and often can be immensely liberating. Because every good word or deed is a catalyst for another. The person who makes your coffee in the morning; the person who manages the landscaping around your building; the person cleaning your office after you've left: these people are your saints. Praise them and you will get it back tenfold. That's the beauty of appreciation. And you can begin right now.

# The New Rules of What If

I F YOU OWN a computer or read the news, you've probably heard of the "two Steves"—Jobs and Wozniak—who founded Apple Computers in 1976. Far less likely is that you've heard of Ron Wayne. He designed the Apple logo and along with Steve Jobs and Wozniak, was one of the original founding partners in Apple. Afraid that their new startup computer company would fail, Ron sold back his 10% stake in Apple for $800, only 12 days after he got it. If he'd held onto that $800 stake, even as a silent partner, today he'd be worth around $22 billion.

Years ago, I had a similar experience, though on a much smaller scale. The firm I worked for, Otec Inc., offered me an opportunity to partner in developing a new online jobs board. Although the idea of creating a startup enterprise was enticing, my position as an executive recruiter was morally fulfilling. Plus, the client relationships and goodwill that I had built over time was not something I was willing to just walk away from. So after some serious consideration, I eventually declined the offer. The new venture went on to become Hotjobs.com and was eventually sold to Yahoo for millions. Some of my co-workers who took the leap of faith essentially retired after that and continue to reap the financial rewards.

When I look back on this choice however, I rarely feel regret. I know that I made the best decision that I could, given the self-awareness and information that I had at the time. Like they say about dogs (there are no bad dogs, just bad owners)—I would say the same is true of our decisions. There are no inherently "bad" decisions, just poor ownership of those decisions. Most of us make decisions with insufficient data. When it comes to making choices, we all do the best we can with the knowledge that we have, and then we must let go of the outcome. Letting go means no regrets, no second-guessing, no self-recrimination. Letting go means being easy on yourself no matter what happens.

One of my clients was recently struggling with a thorny dilemma. She was trying to decide between staying in her current job which offered an enticing promotion, or going back to school for an MBA. "Taking the position feels a bit like jumping into shark-infested waters," she said. "But I fear that coming out of the MBA program, I may never be offered another opportunity like this again. I also know I want to have kids, and getting out of school at 37 with no job and no money is very scary! I once dreamed of having this job title and now that it's in front of me, I'm not sure I even want it anymore." Sound familiar?

In her book *The Joy Diet*, Martha Beck outlines questions to ask when considering any course of action:

1. **Does the thought of taking this step create an inner sense of clarity, despite my apprehensions?** (When a risk is good for you, you may feel apprehension, but little or no confusion.)

2. **Do I feel only fear, or is there also a sense of toxicity akin to disgust?** (Pay attention here: a "good risk" feels like taking a high dive into a sparkling clean pool. A bad risk feels like taking the same leap, but into polluted swamp water.)

**3.** At the end of my life, which will I regret more: taking this risk and failing, or refusing to take it, and never knowing whether I would have succeeded or failed?

I find these questions are useful in discerning fear from excitement, which often can look very alike.

But what if you've already made your decision and it turned out to be the wrong one? That pernicious little voice pops up in your head and begins to chatter loudly: "You saw the red flags and still you ignored it! Boy, you really screwed that one up, didn't you?" To regret past decisions is to reject yourself, and worse, it means overlooking the lessons they have bestowed upon you. It is also a powerless victim state that prevents us from moving forward. Look, we all play the What-if game on occasion; we wouldn't be human otherwise. But the trick is to play the game only going forward, not backwards.

If you must play the *What-if* game, here are the new rules:

## ASK ONLY WHAT-IF QUESTIONS ABOUT THE FUTURE

What if I were to embrace this new opportunity wholeheartedly, what are the potential rewards it may bring? What if I were to take that trip that I've always wanted to do and make it a priority for this year? What if I were to offer my candidacy for that job that I just know I can do better than anyone else in my firm?

## STOP BEATING UP THE YOUNGER VERSION OF YOURSELF

The concerns you had at 25 are very different from those you may have at 35, 45, or 65. We are constantly evolving in body, mind and spirit. So we can rightfully expect that our priorities will change over time too. Don't judge yourself unfairly or keep punishing yourself for some perceived error in judgment. Remember, you were a different person then and you did the best you could. Let it go!

## LEARN TO RECOGNIZE ASSUMPTIONS

Human beings, it turns out, are very bad at predicting the future. We're even worse at predicting what will bring us happiness. So don't assume that you know where a particular path will lead you. Rather, ask yourself "Does this look interesting? Could this be fulfilling or enriching?"

Ultimately, the choice to let go of all our previous decisions (good, bad or indifferent) is a heroic act of forgiveness. But trust me on this: it is the best decision you will ever make. When you are able to give thanks for everything that has happened in your life, then you are truly free.

# Superabundance

As an executive recruiter in the early 90's, I worked mainly on contingency. That is to say, I only got paid when I had successfully placed candidates in a job. Very quickly, I learned to develop a keen sense of who was a prospect and who wasn't. The tendency for most recruiters is to focus only on those few "superstars" who can earn them a nice fat commission at the end of the month.

The problem, for me at least, was that I cared deeply for individuals in the midst of sometimes difficult transitions. I found it hard to cut anyone short. So, I'd pull up a chair, invite them to sit down and then I'd listen to their stories, sometimes for hours. I'd try to think of ways to add value, maybe by making an introduction for them, recommending articles or sharing knowledge. More than once, I was taken to task by superiors for wasting my time on these "no-hopers."

But after a few years in the role, I noticed a slow and steady uptick in my leads through referral. Even if there was no immediate kickback for me, I still invested as much time in people as I could, given the constraints of the job. People appreciated that I made time for them, even when they could do little for me in return. And the goodwill this generated eventually landed me volumes of business.

# GIVE OR TAKE

Most people who are successful share common traits: things like passion, hard work, innovation and persistence. But there's another ingredient that people often overlook, and that is generosity. How much of ourselves are we willing to *give*? Every time we interact with another person, we are faced with a choice: do we try to take as much as we can get, or do we try to add value without worrying what we will receive in return? It's easy enough in our private lives to be givers. Most of us give freely to our friends and family all the time, without ever counting the cost. It becomes more complicated at work where we fear being the sucker.

But according to Adam Grant in his book, *Give and Take*, if we look at some of the most successful people in business—the happiest, the most likely to be promoted, etc—they are generally givers rather than takers. Being a giver at work means you simply strive to be generous in sharing your time, energy, skills and connections with people who can benefit from them. His theory is that nice guys—people who share credit rather than take it, and often do favors for others without expecting anything in return—actually do get ahead in the end.

Unfortunately, most people are deeply scripted in what I call the "Scarcity Mindset." They see life as having only so much, as though there were only one pie out there. And if someone were to get a big slice of the pie, it means less for everybody else. The Scarcity Mentality is the zero-sum paradigm of life. People with a scarcity mindset have a difficult time sharing recognition and credit, power or profit—even with those who help in the production. Not surprisingly, they also have a very hard time being genuinely happy for the success of other people.

The Abundance Mentality, on the other hand, flows out of a deep inner sense of security. It is the paradigm that says "there is plenty of pie and enough to go around for everybody." It results in the sharing of prestige, recognition and decision-making. I often say to people: Whatever you want to attract more of in your life, give it away. Want more respect from your peers, then you have to give more respect to those around you. Want to feel inspired? Inspire those around you. Whatever it is that you feel you're lacking, give it away.

When you put fear and poverty thoughts aside, you become a conduit for goodwill and prosperity. And by giving freely, we prime the pump of our higher consciousness. You don't need to be a Bill Gates or Mother Teresa to make a big difference in the world. It can be as simple as making an introduction for someone, passing on a lead, mentoring a colleague. A belief in a superabundant universe is powerful statement of hope.

# The Myth of Independence

THERE'S AN ALLEGORICAL tale shared across many different cultures, often referred to as the story of "the long spoons." In it, a man is given a tour of heaven and hell. First he visits hell, and what he sees there are thousands of emaciated souls all seated at a massive banquet table. They are starving to death, even though the table is laden with sumptuous food. And the reason they are starving is that each is equipped with only a spoon, but the spoon handle is too long to be able to reach their own mouths. Worse than the actual starvation, is the torment of their frustration.

Next, he visits heaven where a similar scene plays out. Only here, the blessed souls are all well fed and contented, even though they are equipped with the same spoon. How did they accomplish this? Well, they had figured out how to reach across the table and feed the person sitting opposite. They were able to eat all they wanted because they had figured out how to feed one another. All of a sudden, the man understood. Heaven and hell offer very similar circumstances; the difference is in the way that people treat one another. Some people would rather starve than actually give another the pleasure of eating. And if that's the case, they are already living in hell.

This week in the United States we celebrate our national birthday, and the Declaration of Independence that set forth the ideals and aspirations of this newly formed country. As we celebrate our independence, it's worth remembering that we live in a very fragile ecosystem, all parts dependent upon the other for our survival. As John Muir noted: "When we try to pick out anything by itself, we find it hitched to everything else in the universe."

Not only does the melting of the polar ice caps affect the mating habits of penguins, but lo and behold—it also affects our weather patterns! And so it is that the security of "other people" half way around the globe, directly affects our own security here at home. If population growth is not our problem, then it soon will be when the world population doubles in fifty years' time and the demand for basic resources like food and water exceeds supply. Until we recognize the true nature of our *interdependence*, it's unlikely that we will ever know real freedom and security that the founding fathers hoped for.

Sometimes this runs counter to the traditional American ideal of the rugged individual who just wants to be left alone to forge his own path. John Wayne didn't do crowdsourcing to fund his cattle drives, or blog about it on the way ("The hell you say!") But when trouble came a knocking—guess what? It was the "community" who hired Gary Cooper to stand up to the bad guys, paid for by the banker, the butcher, the undertaker and the candlestick maker. It was a collective effort that saw America expand into the great nation it now is. The point is: nobody does it all alone and it would be churlish to pretend otherwise. We need other people to reach our fullest potential as individuals, and as nations.

It is perhaps no surprise then to learn that the new "sharing economy" is slowly changing the way the global marketplace works.

Some of the most successful startup companies in recent years—RelayRides, LiquidSpace, TaskRabbit, Lyft, GETaround, Meetup, Airbnb—understand the "long spoon" concept very well. Human beings do not exist alone in a vacuum, nor do we wish to. By bringing people together, sharing our resources more effectively, we can have a healthier economy, a better quality of life, and feel more connected to the world we live in. Interdependence is not only good for our souls, it's also good for business.

Because we live in a culture that worships independence above all else, we tend to be suspicious of any degree of dependence, seeing it as a tacit sign of weakness. And yet we are all dependent on others in one way or another. Most people find themselves drawn to romantic partners who have different but complementary skills. This is not a sign of weakness, but a sign of intelligence. The myth of independence only promotes isolation and loneliness.

As the saying goes, "If you'd like to change the world, try starting with yourself." A good way to begin is to identify one person who has made a contribution to making your life a little easier, and tell them how this has affected you. Go ahead and thank that person—in person if you can—for all the ways in which they have helped you. Maybe before you get to your desk in the morning, stop and take a minute before plugging in your headphones and connect with someone in your office. Put away your iPhone and look at people's faces now and again. Maybe share some of the details of your personal life, and seek the same in return (but not too much!). Don't be afraid to make the first move. You will feel less scared and less alone because of it.

As John Donne reminds us: "No man is an island." And as it turns out, that is a very good thing.

# Postcards From The Edge

THERE'S A STORY I once heard on the radio and it stayed with me for days. A reporter for *The New Yorker* went to San Francisco to interview the very small group of people who have jumped off the Golden Gate Bridge—and survived. The circumstances that led each of them to hurl their lives away were different, but what they shared afterward was strikingly similar. Each of the jumpers described a moment of clarity, right after jumping, where all they felt was regret. One survivor said that as soon as his hand left the railing, he realized in that moment that everything in his life that he thought was not fixable, was utterly fixable. "As soon as I jumped," he said. "I realized that my life before was perfect." *Yes, it - is*

I sometimes see clients who have given up on themselves. They may not be about to jump off a bridge, but they have fallen into the trap of thinking that their problems are so intractable that no solution or change is even possible. They may be coming to see me under orders, or as a last resort, but they are clearly out of touch with what is possible in their lives. I don't always have the answer, but what I usually do is begin some questions.

# ARE YOU FOLLOWING YOUR HEART?

It sounds very obvious, but are we living courageously with intention, or are we slavishly going through the motions because that's all that we really expect out of life? After all, isn't that what everyone else is doing? There are many things in this life that are important, and a whole lot of stuff that isn't. Knowing the difference is key. The unimportant stuff is infinitely more numerous, and it assails us daily. So we need to be very careful or we can get easily distracted. Being present and accountable to the loved ones in our lives counts a lot. Having the latest Smartphone or the perfect pair of Manolo Blahniks does not. Making something beautiful that others may enjoy or find useful counts for a lot. Going shopping because you're bored does not. Find out what matters to you most, and do more of it.

Much has been made of the passing of Steve Jobs, and rightly so. He lived his life with great courage and intentionality, even in the fading twilight of his recent years. The words used to describe him—rebel, obstinate, perfectionist, troubled—are those we often ascribe to prickly geniuses whose lack of compromise we secretly admire. In his now-famous Stanford Commencement Address, he made the following observation: "Remembering that I'll be dead soon is the most important tool I've ever encountered to help me make the big choices in life. Because almost everything—all external expectations, all pride, all fear of embarrassment or failure—these things just fall away in the face of death, leaving only what is truly important. Remembering that you are going to die is the best way I know to avoid the trap of thinking you have something to lose. You are already naked. There is no reason not to follow your heart."

## ARE YOU LIVING FOR TODAY?

A few weeks ago, my family was robbed of a beloved sister. My brother's wife, Kelly, passed away ten days after giving birth to their first son due to complications from childbirth. She was buried just two days short of their first wedding anniversary. Life transformed in an instant. At 41 years of age, my brother became a widower, and a baby boy will grow up without knowing his mother. Every time I look at him, I'm reminded that nothing is promised in this life, and nothing is owed. You may *think* you know the shape of your life, or how it's going to go, then you wake up one day and that shape changes completely. I share this only as a reflection that every life contains losses, some of them unimaginable. But it's how we respond to them that defines who we are.

After Kelly passed, I watched people pour open their hearts and treasure their loved ones that much more. Hopefully, it does not take for a trauma like this to awaken us from our slumber. We know that everything is impermanent, fleeting. So why do we act as if our time here is infinite? It is not. The value of tragedy is that it awakens us to all those things we had failed to notice before. We learn that it is possible to hold both joy and heartache at the same time. With a little practice and attention, we can learn to savor those everyday moments of beauty, grace, courage and dazzling heroism that surround us. This is the good stuff, and it's right there in front of us.

Imagine for a moment that the life you currently have is taken away from you. Everything in it—gone. And then somehow, miraculously, it was granted back to you.

Now what would you do? *appreciate it!*

# CHAPTER NINE

# Acceptance

*"The mind can make a heaven out of hell,*
*or a hell out of heaven."*

—

**John Milton**

# Square Peg, Round Hole

In his wonderful book *The Element*, Sir Ken Robinson tells a story that I'm sure many people can relate to. In it, a young girl named Gillian is having trouble concentrating at school. The school—perhaps suspecting a learning disability—asks her mother to take 8-year-old Gillian to see a psychiatrist for an evaluation. After hearing from the girl's mother how the girl is always disturbing her classmates, her homework is sloppy and always late—the doctor asked to speak with Gillian alone. Before escorting the mother outside for a private conference, the doctor turned on the radio in the room to occupy Gillian.

As soon as the music began to play, the girl was on her feet. From outside the room, Gillian's mother and the doctor observed for a few minutes as she moved beautifully to the music, dancing around the room, lost in a childlike trance. Then, with a sudden burst of insight, the doctor turned to the girl's mother and said: "Mrs. Lynne, Gillian isn't sick; she is a dancer. She likes to move. My advice? Take her to a dance school."

Happily for Gillian, that is exactly what happened.

She eventually auditioned for the Royal Ballet School in London where she was surrounded by other people who also "liked to move." She graduated, founded her own Dance Company—the Gillian Lynne Dance Company—and soon thereafter met Andrew Lloyd Webber. The rest is history. As a dancer and choreographer, Gillian Lynne has been responsible for some of the most successful musical theater productions in history (ever heard of *Cats*, *Phantom of the Opera*?). She's given pleasure to millions of people and become a multimillionaire in the process. Isn't it fascinating—and absolutely terrifying—to think that somebody else might have put her on medication and told her to calm down? *God damn*

How many of us know people like Gillian? ~~People who are~~ full of energy and wit and drive. People who fidget and can't sit still. People for whom the world is an ill-fitting jacket. As a career coach, I meet these people all the time, though sometimes a lot further downstream than in the above story. Maybe they're out of college a few years and searching for that next big thing. Some of them have been in industry for 20-30 years, doing work for which they seem to have little interest or aptitude. While the verses of individual circumstances are always different, the refrain is all too common.

## I JUST DON'T SEEM TO FIT

One of my clients, Beth, recently confessed to me, "I feel uncomfortable in my job and dread Sunday evenings as all I do is think about how much I loathe starting my work week. I am nervous to talk to my boss about it because I can't be myself in this role." Because Beth is not happy in her career, she went on to tell me that she takes this feeling outside of the office, which brings her down emotionally and often strains her relationships with others.

Another client of mine, Chris, is bored to tears in his job because he has never given thought to what he might actually like to contribute to the world. Deep down, he has an idea about what he'd rather be doing, but he can't seem to get out of his role for one reason or another. Like a manatee, he bobs along from one post to the next, letting circumstances and the tide, carry him to whatever comes along.

Many people carry a vague unsettled feeling of "Is this it?" But finding and uncovering your true talents requires a measure of self-scrutiny and courage that is not always easy to muster. Sure, you may have the aptitude to complete the tasks at hand, but you will likely never shine in a position that does not align your individual gifts with your personal preferences.

What to do?

## 1. Take An Assessment

Part of the formula for having a great career is to be you. Truly you. Just as Gillian had to move in order to think, some of us have to talk to think. If you're a talk-to-think learner, I suspect you talk continuously while learning. You probably sound out ideas and say what's on your mind. Because you rely on other people's responses, you may prefer to work in a group setting.

*Knowing who* you are helps to uncover what you love and what you'll likely be great at. Taking an assessment is one of the best ways to hone in on my clients' values and passions. I often hear a sigh of relief when the results come back. "So *that's* why I am so challenged in my career! I'm in a financial accounting function and my preference is to be the head of human resources." Or, "Wow! I've been in operations for years, when I'm really more inclined to do sales."

This isn't about being rigid and labeling yourself as a specific "type". Rather, it is a way to uncover how you might play to your innate strengths. There are a number of systems out there: Myers-Briggs Type Indicator (MBTI)™, DiSC 2.0, the Kolbe Index, Clifton Strengths Finder. I prefer the HBDI tool which is based on a metaphoric representation of the brain, distinguished by four quadrants of thinking preferences. Once you understand your profile, it will illustrate the way you prefer to learn, communicate, and make decisions.

**2. Find a Mentor**

I've had positions in the past that I was acknowledged in, but that I knew deep down didn't truly speak to me. I was successful at the work but didn't feel fulfilled. I felt stuck, afraid to leave the safety of a paycheck and jump into the abyss of the unknown. What I needed was a mentor—someone outside of my environment who was doing something that interested me.   *Candie*

Speaking with people who are working in fields that you're inspired by, will give you a chance to look under the hood and try the business on for size. Asking people for guidance also helps you to see what is between you and your dream job. How much will it cost and what resources will you need to make the transition? Can you do it alone? What would it look like? What steps do I need to take to move forward? What is at risk if I take this leap? What is at risk if I don't? As simple as it sounds, we all need good mentors. I'm lucky in my life to have several of them. Find one, and do all you can to cultivate that relationship.

**3. Ask for Feedback**

Have you ever noticed at times that what you've been looking for is often right in front of you? Years ago when I worked in recruitment, I had peers telling me that I was extremely helpful when I provided counsel to them. I had a natural ability to listen, be resourceful and helpful. Combine that with a penchant for self-help and I had the recipe for my own personal success. But because those "skills" came easily to me, I was suspect. Now in hindsight, it seems obvious that I've always been wired for coaching.

One of the exercises I conduct with clients involves a "Personal Evaluation" form that they send to their friends and family. Some of these questions include: What do you think are Joe's best abilities, talents and qualities? How would you describe Joe's personality? If this person had his own business, what do you think that would be? What strategic ideas, thoughts, or inventions has this person spoken with you about, if any?

How we see ourselves is often very different from how others may see us. This is why it is useful to ask for feedback from those who know us well. Often the answers can be revealing.

**4.   Partner Up**

Finding others that complement your blind spot is a smart way to excel. Once you understand the dynamics of your own particular style, locate an ally who can bolster up your weaknesses. Research shows that humans tend to do difficult things much better in teams than on their own. Yet, so often my clients blame their weak will when I think they should be blaming isolation. By pooling ideas, you can build momentum in ways that none of your group could achieve alone. Lennon and McCartney. Ben and Jerry. Rolls and Royce. Would we even remember their individual names?

I am really good at helping people to analyze their behavior, but I'm not so good at analyzing their financial portfolios. Knowing what you do (and don't do) well will help you match your skills with a suitable peer who may just be the missing link.

## KNOW THYSELF

All great discoveries are a process of trial and error. So we mustn't be afraid to try different things on for size, and sometimes fail. As Ken Robinson says: "If you're not prepared to be wrong, you'll never come up with anything original." The key to it all is self-knowledge. Just by knowing that you have an inclination to do things in your own unique way, your relationship to—and confidence in—yourself will begin to improve.

Sound impossible? Not at all. For those who are true to themselves in spite of the naysayers, parental expectations, and societal pressures—the world is a vast and beautiful playground. Building an authentic life's work will always be a challenging assignment. But it's worth taking the time to actually figure out what you're naturally good at so that you can simply do more of it.

As George Eliot said: "It's never too late to be what you might have been."

# Becoming a Classic

BACK IN 1985, the Coca-Cola drinks company introduced a new twist on their popular soft drink, the much ballyhooed "new taste of Coca-Cola." But when the coke-drinking public wasn't buying it, the new formula was soon dumped and the old one re-introduced, re-branded as Coca-Cola "Classic." The marketing executives learned very quickly that when Coke tried to be something it was not, it failed miserably.

I was reminded of this last month when I was in Berlin conducting a coaching workshop with my friend and fellow coach, Jerry Colonna. The audience was an energetic group of young European entrepreneurs, all launching new businesses in the face of a shaky world economy. One of the questions that kept coming up was this: How do we create companies that reflect who we are and what we want to achieve?

The simple answer we gave was this: Be Berlin. Don't try to copycat what has already worked in Silicon Valley or China or Brazil. You must divine whatever it is that makes your offering totally unique, and then find clever ways to share it. Certainly, there are businesses that are successful simply by imitating other operations. But typically they are unmemorable, don't last long and make little real contribution beyond the bottom line.

The term used in advertising is Unique Selling Proposition (USP). It is also your brand. As I said at the WIE Symposium last week, whether you're an artist, a business person or a startup tech company, it's worth considering what makes yours unique. Think of the books, art, movies, teachers, people who have had the greatest impact on your life—chances are they were all originals. Somehow a Picasso always "looks like" a Picasso. Salinger just sounds like Salinger. A Quentin Tarantino movie always "feels like" a Tarantino movie. There is no mistaking their fingerprints for another.

A big part of success in any endeavor is learning to sing in uniquely your own voice. You can have the snazziest brochures and the best sales team in the world, but it all means nothing if you don't know what it is that makes you different from the rest. For myself, it was figuring out that I was naturally good at helping people to navigate the corporate world. I had been in their shoes, I had worked at their desks, and I knew what the challenges and points of pain were. And people responded well to that.

If you're having trouble finding your own voice, it's likely that others are too. What are some of the things you can do to help you find it?

## KNOW THYSELF

Knowing your strengths—and weaknesses—is the first step to carving out an identity that is authentically your own. Call a friend if you're having difficulty naming it. Most of us have a simple "knack" for doing something well, but all too often we discount it just because it comes easily to us. We don't trust it. What smart people do is figure out the parts that they're good at, focus on that, and then find other people who are equally good at all the other parts.

Most of the really successful partnerships in the last hundred years are all founded upon this simple premise: Bernie Taupin and Elton John; Woodward and Bernstein; Jagger and Richards. All greater than the sum of their of their individual parts.

## SWIM IN YOUR OWN LANE

It's hard to swim in a straight line when you're busy watching over your shoulder at what the other guy is doing. You know the one that's swimming faster, more easily and more gracefully than you are? Self-comparison is a no-win game, and one of the shortest roads to hell. To wake up from this nightmare, recognize that everyone has their own set of skills, their own set of challenges. And no two paths are alike. Notice when your mind wanders over into the other lane, and then gently bring the focus back to your own stroke. The goal is to embrace your own unique journey. Your potential.

*Thank you*

## KNOW YOUR WHY

What is your purpose? Why are you doing this? Are you doing it out of duty, out of fear, out of desperation? Hopefully not. Work at its very best is "love made visible" as Kahil Gibran once said. Of course, not everybody has the luxury of choosing a job for the love of it, but we must all learn to find the deeper meaning in the work we do, no matter how humble or mundane it may seem at times. You don't need to be building orphanages or saving the rainforests, but you do need to look for (and find) the noble purpose in your work. This is the answer to all ennui and burnout. It's also the single most powerful motivator known to mankind.

In an increasingly homogenized world, it's easy to forget that we are each something truly special. Each of us is a totally unique and miraculous creation—a genuine spark of divine inspiration. Just like Coca-Cola, you have your own "classic" formula. You just need to own it.

# Great Expectations

Earlier this year, I made plans for a September cycling vacation in France. I did my research on the various group tour operators and options, and chose what I thought would be the best one: Provence! For several months in advance, I would visit the website with obsessive frequency, relishing the details of my upcoming trip: the beautiful countryside, gorgeous weather, charming hotels, artisanal food and wine. This would be the trip of a lifetime. And why not? I work hard. I deserve this.

Imagine my disappointment then, when on day two of the trip, I slipped outside my hotel and did a face plant that Buster Keaton would be proud of. (Note to self: never attempt to carry a bicycle down marble steps in cycling shoes.) Sadly, my right knee took the brunt of the fall, and instead of whizzing through vineyards at harvest time, I found myself instead laid-up in a hotel room with a bagful of ice covering a hematoma the size of a golf ball. Goodbye active vacation.

To say that I was disappointed is putting it mildly. This was not the script I had in mind when I booked this holiday. Worse than the physical agony I was in, was the torturous knowledge that I had visited this misfortune upon myself. I didn't even have a good wipeout story to brag about when I got home (though I did think about inventing one). The truth was so much more prosaic, and depressing: I tripped on a friggin' step. Why didn't you just put the bike down, you stupid klutz? Why didn't you take your shoes off? If only I hadn't been in such a rush. If only...

I didn't do much cycling after that, but I sure had a lot of time to think. And when I stopped feeling sorry for myself, I thought about how the problem was not so much my injury, but rather my expectation of how this trip was supposed to go. The greater our expectation, the more we attach to a particular outcome, the more crushing our disappointment when the reality comes up different.  At this intersection of fantasy and reality, we can cause ourselves a whole lot of unnecessary suffering. And when we berate ourselves for tripping up, well, we only make it more painful. Don't Do

I'm not suggesting that we always expect the worst; only that we attach very loosely to our desired outcome. If it happens that way, great! If it doesn't, no biggie, we'll figure something else out. For me, that meant brushing off my crappy attitude and realizing that I still had the privilege of a gorgeous view with plenty of good company. Thankfully, I hadn't broken a leg or poked my eye out, though I easily could have. I soon found myself in the follow van doing what I do best—cheering other people on, and enjoying it.

As an adult, the opportunity for unmet expectations abound. The promotion you had your heart set on goes to someone else. The person you thought was your friend turns out not to have your best interests at heart. The investment you had hoped to close for your business, doesn't come through. The good first date fails to become a second date. That all-nighter that you pulled to save the boss's ass, she didn't even notice it. Low levels of unmet expectations are something that we all experience daily. When you step back and look at it this way, it makes sense to minimize one's expectations of positive outcome in most situations. That way if it happens, you're pleasantly surprised, instead of being permanently pissed off.

Mistakes and setbacks are a natural part of life. A vital step in overcoming setbacks is being able to ask ourselves: "What can I *learn* from this situation?" From my non-cycling holiday in France, I learned to watch my footing when carrying large metal objects. I learned to slow down and really take in the view. I also learned a good dose of compassion. For myself and for others.

But perhaps the biggest lesson of all is forgiveness. Yeah, I screwed up royally. And I'll probably do it again. So I'm not the badass cyclist that I probably like to think I am. That's fantasy Ann. The reality is that I'm an average rider who occasionally trips on steps. When we can let go of the fantasy, reality becomes so much more enjoyable. And when we can forgive ourselves, it's so much easier to forgive others.

Expectations drive so much of our experience of life. We cannot control the outcome of any given event, but we can manage our perception of how things *ought* to be. It's not what happens to us, but how we react to it that really matters. John Milton put it simply: "The mind can make a heaven out of hell, or a hell out of heaven."

I don't believe he left anything out.

# The High Note

WHILE SCANNING THE radio in my car for a good song, I stumbled upon an interview with Paul McCartney. He was funny and engaging, so I stopped to listen for a while. He was asked about his voice, and if, at age 72, he could still sing all those old Beatles songs. His answer was honest and revealing. "Well," he said. "I can't hit all the high notes like I used to, but I've probably got better technique now, and you learn ways around that." Some of those techniques? Changing the melody ever so slightly, letting his back up singers hit the high notes for him, or simply calling upon his audience to fill in the blanks. Music legend Sir Paul McCartney has had to learn that even *he* has musical limitations.

This got me thinking: How much of our lives are spent trying to chase a high note that we are no longer capable of hitting? And what does this cost us in terms of health and happiness? In my own life, I know I hit a high note when I ran my first marathon at 3:26, a personal record for me. It's unlikely I will ever do it again, and that's okay. I have different goals now. But it can be very hard to let go of who we used to be, or who we imagine we still are. We see it all the time in professional sports: the athlete who retires, only to "unretire" six months later. The boxer who wants "one more fight" when everyone around him knows he should have quit years ago.

Most of us are not athletes or professional performers, but we do know what it's like to chase our former glories, and to hunger for that intoxicating high note. Maybe it's the version of ourselves that is 10 years younger, or 20 pounds lighter. Maybe it's the earlier excitement of a new job, or the rush of a new romance. Most of us yearn for these peak experiences, and once experienced, seek to recreate them.

That's not necessarily a bad thing, but it can lead to a lot of frustration and heartache in the present. The problem with chasing only these moments, is that they are generally very fleeting, if they exist at all. And we can miss out on some of the really great moments happening in between. Martina Navratilova said it best: "The moment of victory is much too short to live for that and nothing else."

I knew of one serial entrepreneur who made a killing on his first venture, to the tune of almost $10 million. He went on to create several other successful companies after this, but none as big as the first. Measured against this impossible standard, he felt he was constantly failing, even when, by all outward signs he was a massive success. To his family and work colleagues, he had become a bitter pill who could not enjoy his own success. He was enslaved to the high note, in his case, some arbitrary number below which anything spelled failure. He was Sisyphus, compelled to roll an immense boulder uphill, only to become demoralized every time it rolled back down on top of him.

There are two basic roads that we can travel: one is the road to freedom, and the other is the road to tyranny. The road to tyranny is based on always hitting the high note, and a refusal to accept anything else. It enslaves us to the past, and blinds us to new opportunities in the present. After all, who are we if we can no longer hit the high note? The road to freedom, on the other hand, accepts that all things are in a constant state of flux: our bodies, our minds, our relationships. What we are able to do in our 20s and 30s is very different from what we can do in our 40s, 50s and beyond. And not only is this okay, it is *natural*.

At the root of all unhappiness is our refusal to accept that all things eventually must end: our youth, our beauty and eventually even ourselves. What we are really fighting against is our own mortality, and that is one battle we will never win. But like Paul McCartney, maybe we can learn some new techniques. We can accept that while a relationship has changed, it does not necessarily have to end. We can accept that while a job is no longer as exciting as it once was, it may offer its own kind of reward in the people we meet and experience we bring to it. We can accept that through age or infirmity, a parent is no longer the person we once knew, and try to develop a new connection based on who they are now.

I'm not suggesting we give up or don't stretch ourselves, only that we don't have to be slaves to our past successes (or failures). Graceful surrender to the here and now is always preferable to screeching, or God forbid, ruptured vocal chords. Paul McCartney may not be able to hit the high notes like he used to. All he can do is make friends with the voice he has now, and the many beautiful notes he still can sing. And when the voice cracks, or won't go where he wants it to go, he invites the audience to sing along.

# Alma Matters

THIS WEEK, I will be delivering the commencement address at my former high school in New Jersey. It is a great honor and one that I am proud to accept. As a welcome side benefit, it offers the tantalizing chance to redeem myself for the disastrous speech I gave there as a graduating senior some twenty odd years ago.

On that auspicious occasion, I tripped on my way up to the podium, before delivering one of the most bloated and forgettable speeches in the history of high school graduation speeches. But it wasn't for the want of trying. With typical teenage enthusiasm, I sought to cram in every meaningful quotation I had ever heard, every reaching metaphor and arcane literary reference to drive home my message. Just what that message was, I'm still not entirely sure. The resulting mess was a giant lumbering beast that was dead on arrival: a Thesaurus Rex. In my mind's eye, I can still see my older brother nodding off in the front row, jolted out of his snooze a half hour later by the charitable and half-hearted applause.

In preparation for my "comeback" this week, I started to think about what I would say to my younger self—that anxious, over tanned 18 year-old in the handmade graduation gown. And the first thing I would say is, "ten minutes or less." Nobody has that much attention span, and no 18 year-old has that much to say. Cut, cut, cut! The second thing I would say is, "don't overthink it." While this may feel like the most important moment of your life, it isn't. Not really. Nobody will remember two hours from now what you had to say, and that's okay. The important thing is to show up, do your best, and try to enjoy the overall experience.

We're conditioned to think that our lives revolve around these "big" moments. When we finally win the plaudits, win the crowd, pull the metaphorical sword from the rock. The self-dramatizing teenager in all of us still wants to believe: *This* is the moment that will define me forever. This is the most critical juncture of my life. And you know what? It probably isn't. As I've gotten older, I've learned that life is a *series* of transitions, both large and small, and it's much easier to enjoy it if we hold on very lightly to any desired outcome. There are no final victories, and thankfully, no final defeats either. Some of the other things I would like to say to this teenager?

## BE A GOOD FRIEND (TO YOURSELF)

There will be many important relationships throughout your life, but none as long-lasting or as important as the one you have with yourself. You want to be the kind of friend who is honest and supporting. Who knows and accepts your flaws, but doesn't delight in pointing them out to you. As someone wiser than me once said, "It's hard to be a world beater when you're busy beating yourself up." The way we treat and hold ourselves can have serious consequences, and yet people turn on themselves all the time. Some of the things we say to ourselves, we wouldn't dare say to another. So why would you say them to yourself? You are a fantastic, lovable person, on a journey of discovery. You deserve to be treated with patience, understanding and encouragement. Demand it from yourself.

## AVOID THE COMPARISON GAME

As human beings, we are biologically programmed to look over at the guy in the next lane. Yet nothing causes as much misery as this tendency to compare ourselves unfavorably with others. It's hard to swim in a straight line when you're focused on what the other guy (or girl) is doing. You know the one who is swimming faster, more gracefully and easily than you are? Self-comparison is a no-win game, and the shortest road to hell. The trick then is to gently and carefully, bring the focus back to your own stroke. Recognize that everybody has their own unique set of skills, as well as challenges. The goal is to embrace your journey, your potential. Are you learning? Are you growing? That is all that matters.

## PLAN FOR THE FUTURE, BUT LIVE IN THE NOW

Years ago, there was a bumper sticker that briefly caught on. It read, "Don't postpone joy." For people in a hurry (like me), this is always a difficult concept to grasp. Of course we want more joy in our lives, but it's awful hard to find the time for it when there are so many other competing demands for our time. So we put it off till vacation time, or when we get promoted, or when the kids are grown, or when we retire. "When-then" is the most egregious fallacy of all. It is a mirage. The when is now. Yes, it's good to plan for the future, but the only moment we can fully live and enjoy is the one happening right now. So try to find those small pockets of joy in between the mundane.

*Life* —

And the final thing I would like to remind that callow youth is that all of life is a grand non-repeatable experiment. When we treat it as such, it frees us up from the fear of failure, and opens the door to all kinds of possibility. As John Barrymore once noted: "Happiness often sneaks in through a window you didn't know you left open." Go ahead, and let it in.

*wow!*

# CHAPTER TEN

# Commitment

*"Commitment is an act, not a word."*

—

**Jean Paul Sartre**

# Four Walls of Freedom

YESTERDAY, I SAT on a beach watching my toddler son as he filled a bucket with briny slop, his face a study in concentration. Then a wave came crashing in and swept the bucket away from us. After righting himself and collecting his bucket, he then set about his task again with a singular focus—scoop the sand, fill up the bucket. Repeat.

Sounds dreamy, doesn't it? Yes, it is—but it's not the whole story. As this is going on, I have to constantly remind myself: take it all in, be here now, remember this. Because the other half of my brain is wondering: did I put enough money into the parking meter, when will I have time to finish that report, who's going to mind him on Friday when I go to the city, and what are we going to have for dinner this evening?

It's a lot of work having children, and it's easy to fall into a routine where all I'm doing is worrying about the next thing, and the next thing after that. They create an almost perpetual cycle of chaos in one's life, a thousand trivial and not-so-trivial tasks that crowd out the days, pushing everything else into the background. But my toddler does not care that I may occasionally need to read, or work, or exercise. All that matters to him is *now*. And this is sometimes a useful reminder.

If parenthood has taught me anything, it's that everything in life is a trade-off of some kind. Yes, you will have little moments of pure joy like the one above when all seems right with the world, but then you will lose other things too: things like sleep, hours of unfettered time, freedom to spontaneously wander or just disappear for a few days. It's also taught me that maybe we place too much emphasis on freedom. We imagine that by "keeping our options open" we are somehow liberated, when in fact, too many options can be just as overwhelming as none at all.

## BURN ALL THE BOATS

The story we're told about Cortes is that when he reached the "New World," he gave orders for his men to burn the fleet of ships that had brought them there. Why? Because he knew that given the option of retreat, his men would have no motivation to endure the difficulties that lay ahead. Only when that option was removed could they successfully forge ahead.

We all have our "boats" that we cling to. It could be a job you've outgrown, a relationship that no longer works, an unrealistic fantasy that blinds you to the possibility in front of you. But only by burning the boat—by going *all in*—can we truly know or experience freedom.

In his memoir *Seven Story Mountain*, Thomas Merton describes his rebellious youth and the decision that led him in middle age to becoming a Catholic monk. It was a difficult decision, one he wrestled with his entire adult life. He describes in some detail that exact moment when he finally "burned all his boats" by entering the monastery: "Brother Matthew locked the gate behind me and suddenly I was enclosed in the four walls of my newfound freedom."

A curious way to think of freedom—four walls and a gate! But he understood that only by forgoing all other options was he finally able to follow his one true calling.

I've been thinking a lot about freedom since becoming a parent. Anyone who cares for another person—whether a child, an elderly parent, a sick friend—knows the constant juggle that it is. But we cannot avoid the reality of trade-offs, and we shouldn't try to. Yes, we can do some things, but we can't do *everything*. I understand now that facing and dealing with these limitations has been, and will continue to be, a significant part of my life's education.

What is freedom anyway, except the ability to be fully present in one's life, and to accept each moment exactly as it is. Freedom from the tyranny of choice that provides many options, but gives the gnawing feeling of somehow missing out.

Right now, I have probably fifteen things on my mind, all needing some form of attention. So I have to gently remind myself of what is *really* important. Because if I'm not choosing what that is, then chances are, someone else is choosing it for me.

Scoop up the sand. Fill the bucket. Repeat.

# Adult Education

WHEN YOU'RE A kid, nothing spells your doom quite like those ubiquitous "back-to-school" ads running through the full month of August. Even now, they still have the capacity to conjure that sinking feeling that heralds the end of lazy summer days and a return to normal operations. Once again, I am 9-years-old, going with my mother to get a new school uniform—in my case, an ill-fitting plaid skirt, starchy white shirt, uncomfortable saddle shoes and knee-high white socks. This ritual chore was only marginally offset by the acquisition of a new set of notebooks and pens with which to greet the coming year. For stationery nerds like me, there is always consolation in the crisp new pages of an unused notebook, or the perfectly sharpened point of a fresh pencil.

But education doesn't have to end just because we've stopped going to school. The classroom is all around us. Several years ago while feeling particularly burnt out by work, I made the conscious decision to reframe my focus from "What do I need to do today?" to "What can I *learn* today?" A minor shift in emphasis, but it made a big difference in how I approached my work and life. There's an energy to be found in the learning of anything new. If we're bored, it usually means we've stopped paying attention or stopped learning anything new. You might be able to get some new training within the job you currently have, or you might need to go outside of the office to reignite your passion. But one thing we know about people who live active and engaged lives is that they tend to keep on learning new stuff, even as they age.

## FAIL AGAIN, FAIL BETTER

Back in 2006, Ken Robinson gave an excellent TED talk on the subject of education, entitled "Do Schools Kill Creativity?" It remains one of the most watched videos on the internet, and it's well worth a look if you haven't seen it already. His central thesis is that our current models of formal education are simply outmoded, and do not properly prepare children for the world they will inherit. Children, he says, are ferocious natural learners. And one of the things that makes them such good learners is that they are not afraid of making mistakes; they are not afraid of being wrong. As adults, we are terrified of being wrong and looking foolish—and this greatly inhibits our enjoyment of life and the ability to learn new things. What would we do, or attempt to do, if we didn't worry about looking foolish, or what was "age appropriate?"

To become a lifelong learner is to adopt an attitude of curiosity about the world we live in. A "growth mindset" believes that we can grow our brain's capacity to solve new problems. Stanford psychologist Carol Dweck did a lot of research on learning, and she posits that people tend to have one of two mindsets—fixed or growth. Individuals with a "fixed mindset" believe that their intelligence and abilities are innate and fixed. They don't think they can improve with work and effort. People with a "growth mindset" believe that they can improve themselves through work and practice. Part of this involves granting ourselves permission to do something poorly at first—maybe even to fail hopelessly at it. So teaching children how to handle frustration—essentially learning how to fail better—is a critical component of raising children who are resilient and capable of solving problems.

## SCHOOL OF LIFE

Now more than ever, it is vitally important that we are constantly sharpening our skill set in order to stay competitive and relevant in a volatile jobs market and rapidly changing world. Skills that were cutting edge five years ago are likely out of date now, and the jobs that we will perform in the next decade or two may not even exist yet. What are some of the ways to develop new skills?

Well, most community colleges offer a broad range of evening classes designed to fit around adult schedules. Sometimes it can be fun to have a group of like-minded people learn with you. But you don't even need to engage in formal classes as most of it already exists online. Websites like Khan Academy, Skillshare, OpenStudy and Codecademy do an excellent job of sharing knowledge. Even Youtube has an amazing range of how-to videos that will teach you how to do just about anything. Of course, one of the greatest ways of learning is actually to teach what you already know. Teaching forces you look at everything with beginners' eyes, which can provide clarity and a deeper understanding for yourself.

Our whole life is an education, or at least it can be with the right mental attitude. Sometimes it's signing up for a class, learning a new hobby, or maybe it's just trying something different—turning left instead of right.

We know that physical exercise is good for our bodies, and so it is that "cognitive exercise" is also good for our brains. Staying

*I have an*

cognitively active throughout life—via social engagement or intellectual stimulation—is associated with a lowered risk of developing Alzheimer's disease and depression. But the benefits don't just stop there. As a lifelong learner, you'll be more interesting, charismatic and young at heart. In the words of Henry Ford: "Anyone who stops learning is old, whether twenty or eighty. Anyone who keeps learning stays young."

# Compound Interest

WHEN I WAS in the second grade, my mom took me to our local bank in New Jersey—Hudson City Savings—and opened up an account in my name with fifty dollars in it. I got a little savings book with my name neatly type-written on the cover. I remember feeling suddenly very "adult"—especially now that I was rich!

Every week, or whenever I got some money, I took that little book straight to the bank where a kindly teller smiled at me, and with a hollow *ka-thunk* of his big rubber stamp, recorded my small deposit. Even better than the big inky smudge was the idea that, through the magic of something called "compound interest," the money in this book would continue to grow. Even during the night while I slept. Like Jack's Beanstalk!

I'm not big on New Year's resolutions, but often what I try to do at the beginning of each year, is simply to start saving again. Small deposits, put somewhere safe, that over time, slowly accrue interest. I have five "buckets" that I like to use. You may have more or less. The trick is to make daily investments in each of these, small enough so that we don't feel the pain.

Buckets ✓

### 1. Physical ✓

Do something every day that improves your physical health. Instead of two hours parked in front of the TV or computer screen, can you turn it off and go for a 20-minute walk? Maybe you can cycle to the store instead of driving? Can you take 10 minutes out of your day to stretch—first thing in the morning and last thing at night? I have even started scheduling meetings with clients while walking in the park. We're more apt to begin on time, finish on time, and we get a little exercise in the process.

### 2. Emotional ✓

It's vital that we spend our emotional energy wisely. The ways in which our emotional energy can be squandered are endless: the 24-hour bad news cycle, traffic, unreasonable deadlines, toxic people. Try to surround yourself with people who will uplift and inspire you, not deplete and depress you. If that jerk on the radio makes your blood boil, then why are you listening to him? Spotting the negative influences may take some practice, we have become so used to them. But we don't have to indulge them.

### 3. Mental ✓

The mind is like a muscle and needs exercise too. Can you learn one new thing every day? Big or small, it doesn't matter. Maybe it's somebody's name, a piece of history that you've always wondered about. Maybe you can learn one new word from *The New York Times* list of Most Frequently Looked-up Words? I read recently where author Philip Roth recently bought himself an iPhone: "Every morning I study a chapter of *iPhone for Dummies*," he said. "And now I'm proficient." This from the man who won the Pulitzer Prize!

### 4. Spiritual ✓

Try to get in touch with a "higher force," whatever you perceive that to be. You don't have to meditate for three hours a day, go to a mountaintop, pray to God or even believe in a God. But try to connect with something bigger than yourself for a few moments each day. Even if it's just to stare in awe at nature, or see your humanity reflected in another person. One of the best ways to do this is to practice gratitude daily. Pick out the things in your life that you are grateful for—especially those things you would normally take for granted. The most effective prayer in the world has two words: "Thank you." When you do this, you will find yourself reconnected to the source.

## 5.  Interpersonal

I call this the daily "reach out." It might be someone who has been on my mind recently. An old college friend I owe an email to. Someone I bumped into on an airplane once. An introduction I would like to make for someone. It costs us nothing to pick up the phone, write 4 lines or tweet 140 characters. But it says to somebody, "Hey, I'm thinking about you." If you can add value, or give them something, then so much the better. Nobody can do everything on their own. We need other people, just as other people need us. So try to practice one daily reach out. You may be surprised by the results.

This has been a tough year for lots of reasons. We've seen a bruising election campaign in the U.S., political unrest overseas, a heartbreaking tragedy in Newtown, the incredible destruction of Hurricane Sandy, and a still sluggish economy trying to grow. But every New Year brings us renewed hope, and the chance to begin saving again.

By taking me to Hudson City Savings Bank, my mom knew, even if I didn't, that I probably wasn't going to get rich anytime soon. But she also knew that good habits, practiced regularly over time, help us to grow in the right direction. May all your small deposits yield big dividends.

# Absolute Beginners

Remember what it was like to start in a new job? The rumbling butterflies in your stomach, the sweaty palms, the fixed whatever-you-need grin. I was reminded of this last night when I had dinner with an old friend, and the waitress arrived to take our order. This girl was absolutely beautiful, and as she apologized profusely for not knowing the menu, I could feel her discomfort and overwhelming need to please. "I'm sorry," she said. "This is my first day." We joked a little to put her at ease, and you know what? She was terrific! Throughout the evening, this girl worked her ass off, never once looking tired or like she didn't want to be there.

How sad, I thought, that we all lose this in the end. Eventually work becomes work. But maybe it doesn't have to be this way? Imagine if you approached each new client/prospect/meeting with that same enthusiasm you first brought to the table? How much better and more fulfilling would your work life be, whether you're a CEO or a cocktail waitress?

Remember the unquenchable thirst you had in the early days of learning anything new? The stay-up-till-dawn-figure-it-out excitement that made you feel alive, even though you were exhausted? That is the beginner's mindset. It's also what separates most people who are "good" at their jobs from those people I like to call "genius." By that, I don't mean Albert Einstein genius, but the kind of people in whom you generally recognize excellence the moment you see it, whether they are making you a latte, driving a bus or doing your taxes. It's this clear-eyed ability to see the nuance and newness in each opportunity that will also make you excellent.

In Zen meditation, this is called "practice." Bringing mindfulness to everything you do, so you are seeing each moment with a fresh pair of eyes. "How do you get to Carnegie Hall?" goes the old joke. And the answer is always practice.

The other important aspect of the beginner's mindset is humility: the willingness to look stupid, or risk looking stupid. How much of our time is spent trying to appear "smart"—and how does this cost us in learning terms? Maybe we should try not to be so smart all the time. That way, maybe we can ask the questions we really want to ask, and we can actually learn something new.

As we get older, we tend to forget that learning is a lifelong process. And it is much more than learning from books. I like to think there is no one so ignorant or dull that you cannot learn something from them, if you ask the right questions. To learn is to grow. But it doesn't end at college, age 50, or retirement. If growth is our ultimate goal, then we must commit every day to the discomfort of sometimes being the new kid on the block, or the oldest kid in class. Are you willing to strap on that apron, fix a nervous smile and say: "Welcome! This is my first day."

# Weeds

Ask anyone who owns a garden and they will tell you that weeds are a constant battle—and an absolute nuisance. These pesky, seemingly indestructible super plants will take over any patch of dirt if you let them. You can pull them out or whack them down, but like credit card bills and dental plaque, they inevitably spring right back the minute you turn your back. Plaque and weeds are definitely spiritual brothers.

Last week, I was on my knees in my own garden contemplating this when a thought suddenly occurred to me: this is how our lives are. Constantly under siege by outside forces competing for our precious energy and resources. What do these weeds look like in our own lives? The answer is different for everyone, but I would say anything that distracts you from your primary area of focus might be considered a "weed." If it keeps you from doing what's most important, or stifles your growth and development in any way, then it is almost certainly a weed.

## THE ROOT OF THE PROBLEM

Given the choice to focus or wander, our minds will always prefer to wander. And let's face it, there has never been a better time to be distracted. Television binge-watching on Netflix, Facebook, Youtube, online shopping, fantasy football—these all feel really good in the moment by distracting us from our worries, temporarily easing our anxiety. Most of us are pretty careful with how we spend our money, but far less careful with how we spend our attention. But those hours quickly add up. And how we spend our days is, of course, how we spend our lives. So it requires constant vigilance to rein in our minds and focus on what is really important.

It begins by learning to recognize weeds in the first place, and they can take many forms. These can be negative people, a cluttered home environment, unnecessary time commitments, troublesome or intrusive thoughts. Anything that you are tolerating or simply enduring, may be a weed—and enough of them will slowly choke the life out of you. If you find you are spending too much time in meetings that go nowhere, going on horrible dates, obsessing over someone's Facebook comment, or socializing with people you don't particularly like, then maybe it's time for some judicious pruning. Only by consciously choosing what *not* to care about, can we make room for new growth to occur.

## PULLING WEEDS AND SOWING SEEDS

I recently had lunch with an old friend who had just returned from a seven day meditation retreat in Arizona. Naturally, I was curious what he had learned, so I asked what his biggest insight was at his retreat. "I think I learned how to narrow my focus," he said.

*[handwritten marginalia: "b/c wife b/c O career starting business health New Friends"]*

Then he held up five fingers to illustrate his point. "There's only five things that really matter to me right now: being a good husband, father, health, career and friends." By naming his top priorities in this way, my friend was actively choosing what he wished to cultivate. Everything else would need to be carefully weeded.

Most good gardeners—and I am certainly not one of them—will tell you that cultivating a garden takes time, preparation and patience. It's not enough to just pull the weeds out, you have to actively nurture the plants you want to see grow. That means planting the right thing at the right time of year for next year's bloom, protecting against the weather, insects or other potential hazards. The same could be said of our relationships. Whether we're conscious of it or not, we are constantly sowing the seeds of our future lives. Every conversation, every interaction has a ripple effect down the road. "As you sow, so shall you reap."

Years ago when I worked as a recruiter in New York, I met with many hundreds of individuals in the course of doing my work. There were a lot of meetings that seemingly went nowhere. But even if I had nothing to offer a particular candidate, I made it a point to end on a positive note. I regarded each meeting as a "success" if it led to an ongoing conversation. Maybe something would come up, and maybe we could help each other down the road. And that is often what happened, but not till years later. I didn't know it at the time, but I was actively planting seeds.

Like gardens in the real world, the gardens of our lives require constant care and attention. This means carefully evaluating how and where we spend our time. In his *Seven Habits of Highly Effective People*, Steven Covey suggests, "Do what is important rather than what is urgent." Moreover, it sometimes means setting careful boundaries with friends and family so we don't become overtaxed.

Maybe it means letting go of an old relationship that you have outgrown and is causing you both pain. The golden rule is this: if something makes you come alive, then by all means, keep doing it. But if something just makes you feel dead inside, then have the courage to say "no thanks" or walk away.

One thing is certain, the weeds are never going to fully disappear. The good news is that we can manage them with some careful auditing and intentionality. And if we're lucky, occasionally, we may even enjoy some beautiful blooms.

# Paint Your Masterpiece
## (10 Ideas That Will help To Set You Free)

Last month, I was invited to give a talk at TEDx in the Netherlands. After some initial resistance (it's a lot of work and far away), I decided to take the plunge, and I'm happy to report that it went very well. The theme of this particular conference was reaching your "Full Creative Potential."

I'm lucky to work with a lot of creative people, most of whom are bouncing off the walls with ideas. The trouble is, an idea is not a plan. It's a car without an engine. Execution is ultimately what determines our success in any given venture. And that's what I chose to speak about in a talk I called "Paint Your Masterpiece." Here, in condensed form, I offer you these ten "principles," in hopes that some of them may also be useful to you.

**1.   You will never be ready**

So you don't feel ready, or prepared or smart enough? That's okay, nobody else does either. You don't need to have a Ph.D., or a book published, or an agent, or the perfect business proposal to launch your business or do whatever it is you want to do. You don't need anyone's "permission" either. You don't have to know exactly what you're doing—you simply have to begin it.

What are my natural gifts

## 2. Don't discount the obvious

I got into coaching quite by accident. I was working in recruitment and the thing I enjoyed most about it was meeting different people and trying to offer helpful advice. But that couldn't be a real job, could it? We tend to discount our most natural gifts. It's too easy. Too obvious. So there can be no value in it, right? Well, maybe our true gift is the one we're already giving away for free? Maybe the very important thing you have to offer is right in front of you.

## 3. Execution trumps idea

Ideas by themselves are worthless. Unless you follow through with them. Thomas Edison once said: "A lot of people miss opportunity because it's dressed in overalls and looks like hard work." And if it's worth doing at all, it usually is hard work. Mark Zuckerberg may not have been the first person to come up with the idea for Facebook, but he was the first person to execute on that idea. It's not about the strength of the idea, it's about execution.

## 4. Know your why

Why are you doing the work that you do? What does it mean to you personally? Kahlil Gibran said this: "Work at its very best, is love made visible in the world." Good art and good work—the kind that gets us out of bed in the morning—is usually about the desire to share with others something that we love or value highly. Not surprisingly, it's also what makes some companies great. Share your love of something, and you will never lack for motivation.

## 5. Be who you are

Try to figure out what it is that makes your offering different. The term used in advertising is "Unique Selling Proposition." USP. A big part of success is just learning to sing uniquely in your own voice. If you don't know what makes yours different, you'll just be a pale imitation of someone else. And why would anybody want that? Oscar Wilde said it best: "Be yourself, everyone else is taken."

**6.   Give it away to get it back**

Whatever you want to attract more of in your life, give it away. Want more love and affection in your life? You have to give more love. Want more respect from your peers, then you have to give more respect to those around you. Want to feel inspired? You have to inspire those around you. Whatever it is that you feel you are lacking, give it away. Freely and often. You'll get it back in spades.

**7.   Get stretch marks**

I mean that in the metaphorical sense. Try to expand your own awareness of what you think you're capable of. Anytime you're overcome with fears or doubts or inhibitions, that is your signal to walk towards it. Act directly against your crippling inhibition. If it is the right and reasonable thing to do—then just do it! Give yourself stretch marks. You'll be a bigger and freer person because of it.

**8.   Sometimes you'll stumble**

Ever watch a baby learning to walk? Stand up. Wobble. Fall down. Repeat. This is how we learn any new skill—painfully and awkwardly. So why do we assume as adults that it should be any different? Do not fear making mistakes or looking foolish. Fear not learning anything new.

**9.   Find your tribe**

Yes, you can go it alone, but you certainly don't have to. Try to find other like-minded people who share your passions, energy and enthusiasms. In whatever way you can, seek out and identify your tribe. They're out there. As my favorite poet, David Whyte says: "Your great mistake is to act the drama as if you were alone. Put down the weight of your aloneness and ease into the conversation."

## 10.  Know your value

Never underestimate your own intrinsic value or worth. Unfortunately, this is the one thing you cannot buy, and nobody else can give to you. It's a gift you give to yourself. And the way to do it is by owning the totality of all of your experiences—both good and bad. Every success, every failure, every heartbreak, every crappy job you've ever had—all of it has shaped you into the person you are today. And that person is a masterpiece.

# About the Authors

**Ann Mehl** is an executive coach and career strategist based in New York City. She coaches, speaks and writes about the changing world of work. A former executive recruiter, Ann started her own consulting company in 2005. Since then, she has advised hundreds of men and women from all walks of life. A graduate of Boston College, Ann holds numerous professional accreditations. In addition, she has completed over 50 marathons worldwide. Ann is a founding member of *4Boston*, a nonprofit organization at B.C., dedicated to community and social justice.

**Mark McDevitt** is writer and screenwriter with a varied background in film and television. A graduate of University College Dublin in Ireland, he moved to the United States in 1994 after winning a green card in "the lottery." As a writer and journalist, his work has appeared in *The New York Times*, *The Independent* and *The Examiner*. In 2010, he adapted *The Translator: A Tribesman's Memoir of Darfur* for the screen. In 2015, his biopic about the pioneering investigative journalist *Ida Tarbell* appeared on the Hollywood Blacklist of "best unproduced screenplays." It is currently in active development with Amazon Studios.

Ann and Mark live together in New Jersey with their young son.

Made in the USA
Middletown, DE
11 November 2018